STEPHANIE CALMAN

Confessions of a Failed Grown-Up

Bad Motherhood
and Beyond

MACMILLAN

First published 2006 by Macmillan
an imprint of Pan Macmillan Ltd
Pan Macmillan, 20 New Wharf Road, London N1 9RR
Basingstoke and Oxford
Associated companies throughout the world
www.panmacmillan.com

ISBN-13: 978-1-4050-9213-5
ISBN-10: 1-4050-9213-0

1 3 5 7 9 8 6 4 2

A CIP catalogue record for this book is available
from the British Library.

Typeset by SetSystems Ltd, Saffron Walden, Essex
Printed and bound in Great Britain by
Mackays of Chatham plc, Chatham, Kent

Confessions of a Failed Grown-Up

Also by Stephanie Calman

Confessions of a Bad Mother

To Lawrence and Lydia:
sorry about the swearing.

At least there are now plenty of 10ps in the jar.

No husbands were harmed in the writing of this book.

Much.

Contents

Contents

Shortly after he turns eight, Lawrence seems to turn into an adolescent, reacting to almost everything I say with weary sarcasm, and biting my head off for nothing. At the park one day we meet Billy, one of his friends, with his dad. While the boys play football I ask him, 'You've got four kids. Do they ever go on at you, being nothing but whingey and sarcastic – even when you haven't shouted at them first?'

And he says: 'Yes, they all do – and did. D'you want to know what the secret is?'

'Yes, please.'

'Don't argue with them.'

'. . . ?!'

'Be the Grown-up.'

'Ah. Let me stop you there.'

Introduction

It seems to me that, with the possible exception of driving – and, well, medicine – it's the things in life you don't need qualifications for where you have to have them, and the things you really *ought* to be qualified for that you don't. I don't have an English degree – or any degree for that matter, which always surprises people when they hear I'm a writer. I never even got A for an essay. To take a better example, my old friend Alison went to college to learn to be a beautician and hair-dresser, whereas the most impressive things she's done – raise two children, do up several houses, get divorced and married again, buy a property in France – she's taught herself. You need a certificate to practise as an account-ant or a masseur, where you can't do that much harm, whereas to get *married* – you don't need anything at all. Not even a piece of paper from your psychiatrist saying, *'Stephanie no longer has commitment issues, and can be relied upon to return to the same address each night.'* Or: *'Jeffrey no longer shags everything that moves and can be trusted to go out for the milk and newspapers.'*

As for becoming a parent, the only way to qualify at that is to have had lots of younger brothers and sisters, but with family sizes shrinking you're unlikely to get the chance. Thank God babies don't turn round and say: 'Put me down: you've never done this before.' Or: 'Hang on, you're that girl who tried to have sex on the school trip to Pompeii and eats her children's Easter eggs. I'm out of here.' Mind you, once they learn to talk they challenge you, all right. As my sister said when her son was only one: 'We don't argue because he hasn't got enough words yet.'

And once they do, you'd better hope you've got the hang of it, because they inform you on a daily, if not hourly, basis that you're failing. You're mean not serving ice cream three times a day, unfair switching the light off at 8 p.m, and cruel because you gave their brother a biscuit, which shows you love him more, and so on and so on. But they don't question your actual credentials. And it's the same with Grown-upness in general. Perhaps it should be like Kumon maths: you can't move on to the next stage until you've mastered the previous one. Because no one comes along and says, 'Sorry, we can't sell you this suit/house/wedding package/ insurance policy/car: you're just too immature.'

Maybe they should.

1 It's Not Fair

A Thursday morning. I'm sitting in my GP's surgery, discussing the possibility that I might have insulin resistance, which can lead to diabetes. I'm hoping to blame it on heredity, but it's starting to look a bit inescapable that the amount of buns, chips and toast I'm eating is too much for my pancreas, which I regard as a sort of magic organ capable of absorbing enough carbohydrates to sink a ferry. I'm not eating the buns, chips and toast in front of her – in fact, she's never seen me eating, which makes it very tempting to lie. This is how people who are coughing their lungs up onto the surgery carpet can claim to be victims of passive smoking; they haven't been caught with the twenty fags actually in their mouth.

'I do eat some rubbish, obviously,' I begin. 'But – you know, not *that* much.'

She looks at me non-committally.

'And how much exercise do you take?'

While I'm thinking what to answer to this, I try to work out whether, if I do get diabetes, there could be an upside. Sympathy? Almost certainly. A colourful newsletter from the British Diabetic Association or other supportive body? Hm. That doesn't seem enough. On the other hand, what I've got now is a potential ban about to be imposed on all my favourite foods, without anything pity-inducing to whip out at dinner parties, like a syringe.

She's waiting for an answer.

'Well, I walk Lawrence to school, as you know,' I say. She knows I'm not making this up; she often sees us arriving since she has children there too. And it does take twenty-five pretty brisk minutes. Unfortunately she also probably sees Peter arriving on the days he takes him, which in any given week is at least two. Then there is the bus. It only goes halfway and is therefore almost pointless, but Lawrence forces us to take it on the days we leave early enough, reducing the walk to ten minutes at the other end.

'Hmm, you really should do more.'

'Right. Right. Of course.'

'Don't take lifts or escalators. Use the stairs.'

'Ah, well, that's just it you see. My physio said to avoid them since I fell over that time and injured my knee.' This happens to be true, but I can tell the moment I say it, it sounds like an excuse. She moves on.

'And you could lose about ten pounds.'

Oh, this is, like, so unfair! I'm not fat. I've got a BMI of twenty-one, *so there*. And she's very tall – and *thin* – a beanpole, I'd say, so she's obviously biased. I mean, you know thin people – they always think everyone else is fat. I look at the floor. I don't eat *that* much crap. Why is she picking on *me*, anyway?

'It's really difficult,' I say. 'When I went back on the Pill to try and deal with my awful periods' – surely this will get me *some* sympathy – 'I put on weight, and, as you know, having polycystic ovaries makes you put on weight anyway, so . . . it's really difficult.'

She looks at me levelly.

'You really need to stop being so negative.'

This is awful. I've gone back in time, to the horrendous slimming club I joined when I was sixteen. Ten weeks in a grim church hall during which I went from being pretty keen on food to *obsessed*. It wasn't helped by my boyfriend at the time telling me to diet. Just thinking about him makes me boil, not to mention the fact that I'm already on the damn cholesterol medication. What more do they want? In a minute she's going to make me stand in the corner. This is *so* unfair. I gave up smoking. Why can't I have the foods I like? I remember a visit to a doctor, twenty years ago, when my cholesterol was first measured. She looked up from the results and said, 'You realize you'll probably have a heart attack before you're thirty-nine.'

So I went to a café and had a black coffee and a cigarette. There's nothing like making someone feel completely powerless to motivate them to give up on life. It's situations like this that make people turn to chips.

The doc attempts a smile.

'Look, just do your best,' she says. 'OK?'

But my face has heated up and I can hardly look her in the eye. I've got smaller and smaller like Tom Hanks at the end of the film *Big*. Even as a voice in my head is saying, *'Come on: you're the SAME AGE'*, I want to moan, *'But it's not FAIR.'*

In the end I mumble something that's meant to be 'Righto!' but probably comes out as: 'Yes, Miss; sorry, Miss. Can I go now?' To avoid looking at her I pretend to look for my keys, even though I know they're in my bag. She is in fact a very good doctor; I ought to be grateful. After all, my GP when I was a teenager was a chain-smoking mountain of a woman with a cough that could have powered the Industrial Revolution.

But do I appreciate this? No. I fold my arms and moan. I've just been turned back into a podgy adolescent with a horrible boyfriend – all because I might have a condition commonly associated with the very old. It just stinks, that's all. And you know what the worst part is? More and more of my life is starting to feel like this. I mean, surely, by the time you get lines on your face the teenage angst should start to recede. I mean, come *on*. That is so – *lame*, or whatever the word is this week, and don't blame me because I'm bound to have got it wrong, so – *whatever*. I should have been a Grown-up by now. I'm just not. I'm sorry – *OK*?

2 What Is a Grown-up?

It's generally accepted that growing up is a Good Thing, but what *is* it, really? And how do you know when you've done it? More crucially, perhaps, how do you know when you haven't? I've always thought that a Grown-up is someone who manages not to eat all the icing off their cake in one go, but I think there may be a bit more to it than that.

So what is a Grown-up? And how do you become one?

I ask Peter, who as well as being my husband is my honorary elder brother. He says: 'It's knowing when to pick your nose.'

'What?!'

'You don't stop doing it as an adult, do you? You just stop doing it in front of other people.'

'I was kind of hoping for something with a bit more – you know. Depth.'

'You don't want Depth. This is *True*.'

'Yes – to the gender that picks their nose all the time, for example, in their cars. Why do men do that?'

'You're not writing about men, you're writing about being a Grown-up.'

'*Not* being a Grown-up. Blimey! Don't you listen to *anything*?'

'Don't start getting shirty with me. I picked up the children today.'

'Oh, here we go. I learned to kiss when I was thirteen.'

'Yes, we all know how advanced you were.'

'The difference is, I didn't carry on into my twenties going on about it.'

'And I hung up the swimming things.'

'Men *are* obsessed. I was in a bar once, with a friend. And a man at the same table started picking his nose. It was disgusting!'

'Urgh!'

'I know. I asked him to stop and he wouldn't, so we left. I really felt sick.'

'Storming out, though; that's a bit over the top.'

'We didn't "storm out". There was nowhere else to sit.'

'Oh.'

According to him I'm always 'storming out' – one

reason I'm not a Grown-up. Except I'm not. I only do it with him, and anyhow these days I only storm into the next room, because when I did once storm out of the house it was raining and I didn't have my key. So I had to wait quite a while before asking to be let back in. Come to think of it, maybe that *is* a Grown-up characteristic: Thinking Ahead.

'So: anything else?'

'I had a tutor at Sussex who picked his nose.'

'Not that!'

'What, then?'

'Being a Grown-up, for God's sake!'

'All right, all right. Don't bark at me.'

'Well?'

'Seeing the other person's point of view.'

'Now, that's good.'

'And being willing to compromise.'

'Great!'

I've only been on the Big Question for an hour, and already I've got the answer. This is Excellent.

'You know the biography of Alec Issigonis you gave me for my fiftieth birthday? And the one about Patrick MacNee?* They're both presents I would have loved equally at eleven.'

---

* Steed in *The Avengers*.

'So what, you're saying you *haven't* Grown-up?'

'I'm saying I'm still into the same things.'

'Why can't you be? I loved eating cake mixture when I was young, and I still do.'

'I thought I'd have to give up all my interests, like toy cars and so on, because I associated them with being a child, I suppose.'

'And you thought you had to let go of them to move on.'

'Also . . .'

'What?'

'I was beginning to look at pictures of women, and I couldn't see how I could do both.'

'What, enjoy naked women *and* cars? Er! Where have you been? Oh, naked women and *toy* cars. Maybe that's a bit . . .'

'And I was definitely aware, as I got to about twelve, that no one else around me was building models out of kits.'

'Cars, not women, we assume. Where did you see pictures of women, anyway? Up there in the respectable bit of 1960s Sheffield.'

'I found a copy of *Parade* magazine on the bus.'

'*Parade* magazine! Ah, that evokes a bygone era.'

Parade was part of the pubeless empire of retouching, what became later, with improved technology, airbrushing.

And now we have Photoshop. But I digress. There's quite a thin line between a nice number of toys and Too Many. A man who's kept a few boxes of childhood favourites – that's kind of sweet. A man living alone with several glass cabinets full: sad. Come to think of it, it's the display case that does it; well, that combined with the likelihood of dandruff and crispy sheets. To know what God thinks of adult toy collectors, you only have to look at Al of Al's Toy Barn in *Toy Story 2*. And the only toy who *wants* to spend his life in a museum is Stinky Pete. But let's not forget women can be weirdos too. *Women Can Be Weirdos 2: Say Hello to Teddy*. Thirty-five-year-old females who have pyramids of cuddly toys on their beds; if I was a bloke I'd be just a teensy bit put off. My sister worked with a woman whose boyfriend – amazingly, she did have one – brought a different teddy to meet her after work every day.

'When I was at university, a girl came to my flat and saw my car collection and said, *"That's a bit weird"*.'

'Lucky I came along, then.'

'She was Australian.'

'Oh, well then.'

He didn't shag her, he claims because he didn't fancy her, not because she didn't want to take her clothes off surrounded by rows of very small delivery vans.

'But then I met a brilliant electronics student who had loads of cars and was completely unapologetic.'

'And who had tremendous BO.'

'No! He was cool.'

'If you say so.'

In order to further delay grappling with it myself, I decide to put the question to my sister. Of the two of us she was always the Sensible One – and not in a dull way. This, despite being three years younger. Also, she has matching bedside thingies in her house with integral lights, all coordinated, while we have a wicker table on one side of the bed left over from a garden furniture set that we had to throw away when the children jumped on the chairs and broke them, and a chest of drawers on the other with drawers that don't stay shut. And she has alcoves in her dining room *with their own lights*. We don't even have alcoves, unless you count the space between the bookshelves where Peter once found two sausages.

She says: 'Ask me in ten years.'

'Ha-ha! That's not actually that useful. Anything else?'

'It's when I've dealt with something tricky not too badly, i.e. not been whiny, manipulative or bossy. But it's only afterwards I think, *That went quite well*. You never think so at the time. But my Inner Age is twelve.'

'That's very precise. How do you know?'

'Because I like to talk and eat chocolate all day with my friends.'

'A man came on the radio this morning reviewing Easter eggs, and said, *"I'm a Grown-up: I like dark chocolate"*.'

'Well, *nyeah* to him. Sometimes when I'm driving, I think: *Wow, I'm driving!*'

'Eeeek! So do I! But I didn't want to tell anyone in case—'

'It sounds ridiculous.'

'I know.'

'Maybe I won't put that in.'

I like the Inner Age idea; everyone should have theirs measured and stored on a National Database. It'd only be a problem for those with something to hide. And it'd be ideal when choosing a mate. If your target spouse was revealed to have an IA below about eleven, you'd know to steer clear.

I think, maybe, you can tell people's Inner Age from their attitude to Going Away.

The first time I ever went abroad was to France with

the school when I was seven. I just couldn't believe there was a whole country where people automatically spoke in a different language. And I couldn't understand how they managed to answer so quickly, when they had to translate everything from the English in their heads.

People who travel all the time, who don't even take home the spare shampoo from their hotel, or pick up their business-class toiletry packs, I reckon have an IA of about forty. And when I get to go anywhere, I pretend to be forty. When I had to go to Manchester for work not that long ago, I checked in very straight-faced, and ordered a paper for the morning. Then I went up, and Rebecca, the girl I was travelling with, came in to compare rooms.

'You've got a Superior Room,' she said, straight away.

'How do you know?'

'You've got a table and two chairs.'

'Ooh, yeah.'

'And how many chocolates do you have on your pillow? Oh, none!'

'Four.'

In the time it took her to come next door, I had eaten them.

'And look at this!' I showed her my shampoo and bath stuff – leaning on a rack in test tubes.

'That is so cool! And two sinks!'

'One for each hand.'

It was so gorgeous there wasn't even a kettle.

I took the test tubes home, and – though it was hard for me – gave them to the kids. The writing paper I added to my foreign and hotel stationery collection, which goes right back to the first piece I ever saved, from my dad's trip on the *QE2* when I was four. It has a picture of the ship on it. I also have a small but treasured collection of airline toilet bags complete with all their pots and tubes and little combs. An opportunity to add to it can occur at the most unexpected moments. Peter's friend Don travels a lot for work. One day, I was round there for some reason and the subject came up somehow. I think Kate, his wife, was bemoaning the number of airline toilet bags cluttering up the bedroom. And I said, 'I *love* airline toilet bags.'

So she went to get me some. And while she was handing me three of these things, Don came in.

'What are you doing?' he complained.

'I'm just giving Stephanie some of these – things.'

'But they're my airline bags!'

Immediately I recognized a kindred spirit. Well, a man who brought home every single one he was given – how could he not be? But my need to bond with the kindred spirit conflicted with my desire to have the bags. After all, they were Virgin Upper Class: black canvas with *mini glass pots* of toner, eye gel and face cream. I said, 'Look, if he needs them . . .'

'Oh, don't be ridiculous! Don, you've got hundreds of these things.'

'No, I haven't.'

I watched with deepening empathy: a man in a fairly expensive suit, a fund manager, in fact, battling to save his collection of airline toilet bags.

'They're just like us,' said Peter afterwards, when I told him. He watched me unpack and admire the little glass pots. 'And you're going to use those, are you?'

'Well . . .'

He watched, shaking his head, as I put the pots back in the black canvas bag, zipped it up, and stored it carefully in the drawer under the bed with the others.

3 Part the Red Sea If You Have To

Assuming that we all, consciously or unconsciously, base our idea of maturity to some extent on our parents, I realize, somewhat uncomfortably, that I've probably spent the last twenty years copying them both. But instead of getting the best of both, it looks as though I may have got the worst.

When my mother was young, girls left home pretty much only to get married, so when she moved out and rented a studio *on her own*, her parents thought she – and they – had failed. Both she and my father had to flee their upbringings to gain independence but being artists, neither of them could ever have become proper Grown-ups anyway, which explains, according to Peter, why I had no obvious adults in my life from whom to get the idea. His parents, on the other hand, conformed far more to the adult norm. His mother wore an apron – an item my mother wouldn't have known what to do with. And his father smoked a pipe, the very idea of which conjures up an image of confidence and more confident times, when Britain had a manufacturing base and a third of the map was pink. Given the same prop, my father would have used it to keep paper clips in.

Because he clearly inherited his father's attitude to practical matters is one reason I looked up to Peter from the word go as a Grown-up, or at least more Grown-up than I am. Apart from when he won't immediately solve the exact problem I've dumped on him at that particular moment, he relishes a three-dimensional challenge. Things that need fixing intrigue and fascinate him; when he sees a loose door handle, he actually moves towards it, as opposed to adopting the three-pronged Calman approach: waggle, frown, walk away. Of course, when he can't mend something, he has to contend with my childish disappointment, as if *he's* the defective model that should go back in the box.

On this point, he and Claire's husband are engaged in a tacit and entirely non-mature contest to see who can be my mother's favourite son-in-law. But since the Other SIL is Jewish and has DIY-phobia – according to him, it stands for *'Don't Involve Yourself'* – Peter always wins. OK, he tries to make up for it by *tidying*. But, you know, it's hardly the same thing. On the other hand, it's always been pathetically easy to impress my mother with a screwdriver, since she regards anything technical with a fear and suspicion bordering on the mediaeval.

To her, How Things Work is like the Immaculate Conception to Catholics, a mystery that Cannot Be Solved, and one definitely not subject to question by a lay person. To give you an example, she rang me once to say she couldn't operate her new tape-recorder. So I said, 'Well, what are you doing?'

'Well, pressing *Play*, obviously. And . . .'

'And . . .?'

'*Fast-forward.*'

So for anything that might require deployment of a screwdriver, her view is you'd better Get a Man In. And as you can probably tell from that, she generally needs to. Replacing a tap washer? Get a Man In. Opening a bottle of wine? Get a Man In. She looks upon plumbers, carpenters or any male purporting to carry a toolbox, as gods. Years ago, when we still shared a dwelling, she bought me a lamp which needed two wires screwing into a fitting, and she said we'd have to Get a Man In. We didn't know anyone with a toolbox, so she thought we should ask the bloke up the road who made architectural models and props for TV commercials and might

– just – have had the level of technical expertise needed to push two wires into a hole and tighten the screws. When I refused and did it myself, she looked at me in a new light, the way Captain Kirk used to peer at female aliens who, due to the limits of the budget, had had to appear in human form but were invariably spotted as abnormal due to being up for snogging William Shatner. Maybe she was wondering who my real parents were.

While Mum has always tended to overestimate how complicated or difficult something is going to be, my father would underestimate. No, it was more a case of: 'Obstacles? Get out of my way.' He just wouldn't have them. Once, despite having never baked anything before, he decided to make chocolate brownies. He refused to be discouraged by the fact that he had no eggs, nor could he be bothered to go out and get some. (You see the greed v laziness gene rearing its head, more of which later.) No, he just made them anyway. And naturally they came out flat. And what he said when he saw them was, 'They're very good as biscuits.'

It sort of sums up his whole approach.

He was ambitious, and when not working loved to travel. But he was quite childish about food, and even in New York and London, refused to have anything to do with Indian or Chinese. Even when he went to the Caribbean it had to be the French part, in case he was forced to eat anything he hadn't already had in Paris.

He might just possibly have been influenced by his mother – not someone who could see the point of changing countries, it seemed, unless you were fleeing. The first time he told her he was going to Paris, she apparently said, 'What for?'

Interesting, isn't it, that Jewish Mothers produced such bold entrepreneurs. That they were allowed out of the house long enough to build Hollywood is impressive. And you can just hear Moses' mother calling out, as the column of Israelites snaked over the horizon: '*OK, part the Red Sea if you have to. But don't forget supper on Friday.*' Then, as soon as he got to the other side: '*You can't call? What kind of a Promised Land is it, with no phone?*' As for Forty Days in the Wilderness, I reckon Jesus had to tell his mother that so she wouldn't join him. Actually he was in Florida.

Anything Dad fancied doing, he'd have a go – like Indiana Jones trying to fly a plane in *Raiders of the Lost Ark*: 'How hard can it be?'

I remember, when still at that age when you think they know everything, asking him how a jet worked. He said: 'It – goes much faster.'

Where the difference between his attitude and my

mother's really showed up was when, some years after they'd split up, he announced his intention to open an art gallery.

'What, and sell pictures?!' she gasped. 'But you've never run a shop before!' She was so staggered by the mad recklessness of it, she practically had to lean against a wall for support. Mind you, he was going to do it with my stepmother, whose approach to profit and loss was even more dreamlike than his. He insisted, 'A shop's just a building with things in it and a till.'

At this, Mum's brain was practically exploding.

'Well, you'll *have* to go on a book-keeping course.'

'Don't be ridiculous! There's nothing to it.'

There turned out to be quite a bit to it. He did indeed open a shop, and did indeed not make any money. I used to wish he could have been Richard Branson or a billionaire Asian, but he'd never have managed the hours. When he got bored sitting behind the desk, he'd go off for a cup of tea, leaving scrawled notes on the door that said: *'Back in 5 mins – probably.'*

As I say, I'd hoped to have inherited the best of his and my mother's characteristics, but sadly you can't – so far, anyway – genetically modify yourself. When I contemplate doing something new, I worry way too much and think of reasons not to do it, like my mother, then end up jumping into it without proper preparation anyhow, like my dad. Yes, I started www.badmothersclub.com with no knowledge of the internet, and yes, I still don't have a business plan. Or even an office. And the only thing I seem to have inherited from both of them is the ability to gaze out of the window for a great deal of the day.

My friend Mark says you grow up when your parents die. Or rather, you're supposed to. He was at school with a boy whose father died, when he was thirteen, and he sort of turned into a man overnight.

'His father had pissed the family money up the wall, and then died too early, and he just decided there and then that he wouldn't leave his family in the lurch like that.'

Then I remember an interview I read in the paper recently, with a man of about twenty whose mother had just died of a drug overdose. The family have every problem Social Services could ever imagine. They make the Gallaghers of *Shameless* look like the Von Trapps. But this eldest son has made a decision.

'I realized that if I didn't look after them,' he says, 'no one would.'

So he's given up drinking, got his act together and become Chief Carer.

'Wow,' says Mark.

'Wow indeed,' I say.

So does losing a parent really make you Grow Up? Even one who hasn't inspired you to do so by being crap?

When it happened to me I felt it did.

I was thirty-three at the time, and still waiting to take control of my life.

I was a former waitress, secretary, on-off writer and shop assistant. I'd only ever had one full-time job, which – top marks for fashionableness – was on a music paper, but, no marks for fashionableness, one that nobody read. I left intending to be snapped up by one of the national newspapers who would pay handsomely for my unique insights into Contemporary Youth Culture. Nobody snapped. So I went to America to be an Independent Traveller and observe crystalline vignettes of Life which I would turn into beautifully wrought short stories like John Cheever's. But I only got as far as Connecticut. I hated travelling alone, got cripplingly homesick, and when I got word that my grandfather had died, returned gratefully home.

Periodically my father would take me out for lunch or tea and deliver stirring pep talks about the Jewish Spirit of Determination and Not Giving Up. For him, being not very good at drawing had turned out to be the ultimate blessing in disguise; what he was all along was a writer who used pictures to help the words along. With nothing going for him but a talent described by one of his tutors as 'very latent', he turned himself into a cartoonist and invented a brand-new style.

The only things I'd achieved by myself – i.e. without his help – apart from the job I no longer had, were an interview with a band for a magazine on cassette, which struggled on for about four issues before closing, and the nightclub listings for a new weekly which declined to pay me. I was only half-Jewish, so where was the Jewish Spirit of Determination and Not Giving Up? Clearly in the wrong half. I was like an electric car with my father the battery; each time I'd set off seemingly with plenty of juice, then run out and have to be recharged. If I didn't get my act together, I'd be forty, with him still taking me to parties and saying, 'There's the editor of *Blah Blah* magazine. Go and talk to him. He might give you some work.' I hadn't even had the sense to buy myself three extra years by going to university.

Most humiliatingly of all, I had failed to graduate in one very basic respect; I didn't even own my own home. My sister had moved out to live with a man I introduced her to. Even the extra delicate girls I knew, the ones who couldn't drive, or were terrible with money, even

the virgins who still had teddy bears on their beds –
even they were settling down. Eventually all my friends
had found men with whom to buy flats or even houses.
Meanwhile I stayed on in the building my parents
moved into the year I was born. The low rent and
central location had blinded me to the fact that,
unmaintained and uncleaned, it was gradually evolving
into a well-appointed, middle-class slum.

When Claire was still there, it was amusing. Its
idiosyncrasies made a handy talking point, like a bon-
kers or colourful pet. Every room had a feature which
had been cocked up. Bathroom and kitchen had both
been carved out of the original kitchen, but instead of
making two normal-shaped rooms, the wall turned a
corner in the middle to make a shallow V. The 'breakfast counter' along one side was incredibly narrow, so
that you ate your boiled eggs and Hovis with your nose
virtually touching the wall. There was a table, a black
one made of some abnormally heavy substance, with
flaps. It had to be positioned very precisely: an inch too
far one way and you couldn't get the fridge open; a few
millimetres the other way and you couldn't get out of
the room.

My parents had never bought a sofa or any comfortable chairs. There was just the thing my mother called
a 'divan', long and rectangular with no back or arms,

against the wall. It was quite deep, so if you sat with your back against the wall for support, your legs stuck out, making you feel much younger, like being on the mat at school. It was always called 'the divan', and I was taken aback when it dawned on me years later, with the wisdom of the advancing years, that it was just a bed.

When I was twenty-two and Claire nineteen, we rebelled violently against our upbringing and bought a sofa. It seems hard to believe now, the reverence with which we gazed at it from our sitting positions on the coffee table. It was over a month before we sat on it.

But it wasn't just the furniture I noticed in other people's houses that reminded me how unGrown-up I was. They were living in a different climate. Like natives of a remote island who have never seen photography, we were the last of the generation to grow up without central heating. When they moved in, my parents had installed a solid fuel stove which heated the sitting room very efficiently and left the rest of the place freezing cold. The bedrooms had very heavy, oil-filled, plug-in 'portable' radiators – they could be pushed across the carpet if you threw your whole weight against them – which were in addition expensive *and* extremely slow to heat up. The stove ate hundred-weights of anthracite, delivered to the second floor by black-clad men who heaved the sacks over their shoulders into the coal box opposite the front door. The coal box was huge – three foot high, and, like Barbie, had no opening down below. The only way to get coal out of it was by Caesarean. You had to lift the immense, hinged lid, spread newspaper over the side, and, grasping the hod firmly in both hands prior to describing a scooping motion, stretch your torso up as far as possible and lean in. Apart from obviously coming out with some coal, the aim was not to fall in.

Because we had to do this at least once a day in winter, nothing was supposed to be kept on top of the coal box. But there was no room in the hall for even a small table, so things were: a spiny legged lamp with raffia shade . . . artwork, ingoing and outgoing . . . newspapers, magazines, hats, gloves, bills and numerous things left behind by guests that couldn't be put away in case they came back for them and they couldn't be found. All this stuff would accumulate and have to be removed daily – more, if you'd forgotten to keep a spare hod full. You had to lean in, do one big scoop and retreat before breathing in too much black dust. It goes without saying that these were the rare occasions we all kept our mouths shut. Coming in alone, and God forbid if you had pulled, meant a lonely fumble in the dusty blackness, knowing that the scooping would wake everybody up. However pissed or exhausted, you had to reload. When the coal had burned right down, i.e. was red hot, the heat blasted volcanically out of the top and the risk to facial hair was at its greatest. And although I had, and have, a problem in that area, I never considered stubble-burning a reliable method of removal. It was only by staying well out of the way during loading that my father managed to keep his beard. Our former nanny Shea, now over eighty, still has to paint on her eyebrows. But if you shirked this duty, the stove would *go out*.

The trick was to choose the right moment to interrupt the flow of things to disappear down the hall and dive into the box. Men who gave up waiting and crashed out before I reappeared must have been baffled. Perhaps they thought I was loading an unusually labour intensive kind of contraceptive. But at least it meant they'd still be alive at breakfast. You didn't want to wake up to a man who was stiff, and not in a Good Way. All in all, it seemed a lot of trouble to go to, just to heat one room.

When Claire and I finally abandoned the stove we still didn't put in central heating. We couldn't afford to pay for it in one go and were terrified of debt. So we got a Calor gas fire on wheels with a cylinder inside that we trundled from room to room. It was less onerous than the stove, but guests had to be discouraged from making any sudden moves. If they changed rooms without warning, they had to wait while one of us went to fetch the heat. After the winter of 1986, when we lived mostly in one room, running down to the chippy to buy supper, and then jumping shivering back into bed, I decided I must have a relationship at all costs. I didn't mind what he was like, as long as he had central heating.

Peter went one better. After our first night together, unable to face getting undressed again in that temperature, he bought me a proper fire. He then further demonstrated his commitment to our mutual happiness by nailing a piece of hardboard over the hole in the wall where the rain came in. He even covered it with lining paper and painted it to match the room. (And people ask why I never demand Valentine's Day flowers.) When I stayed the whole weekend at his flat for the first time, and we sat at opposite ends of the sofa reading the papers, I thought: *Grown-up at last! This is really, really It.*

But of course it wasn't. Or rather, it was – *It*. It just wasn't the end of all my insecurities, just the start of a whole load of new ones.

4 More of an Experience

My father died at the cinema. It wasn't the first time he'd caused a scene during a film. As children we were frequently reduced to quivering embarrassment as he bought the cheapest tickets, in the front five rows, then moved back. We would then wait anxiously until the manager appeared and asked us to move forward again – 'These are the *five* shilling seats, sir,' and Dad would shout: 'There's no one bloody sitting there!' as we sank lower and lower in our seats.

He had a coronary in the middle of *Carlito's Way*, at the point where Al Pacino cuts someone's throat. For someone so used to causing scenes, he went unnaturally quietly. But when his girlfriend raised the alarm, the film was stopped, the Empire was closed and he was borne through Leicester Square with sirens past the astonished crowd. I don't know if anyone asked for their money back. At least he had lived to see one-price seating. I've still got his ticket, which says on the back:

More of an Experience

'*UCI – More of an Experience*'. It's not often you get a slogan that delivers.

In films and TV dramas people always get The News when they're doing something very mundane. They're sitting round the dinner table or something, and there's a knock at the door, then a cut to a police-person standing outside. We were in a wine bar at the time. At the actual moment it must have occurred, I'm pretty sure I was laughing. I was with Peter – no kids then, and Steve and David, two friends from work. They came back to my place, and we got fish and chips. Claire, who was in bed with a cold, got up and joined us in her dressing gown. We were not at all keen to answer the phone. It must have rung six times before we heard it, and Debby, his girlfriend's voice, on the answerphone. I picked up and she told me he was dead. I said: '*Stay there – I'm on my way. It'll be all right.*'

It'll be *all right*?? I might as well have said, '*What on earth—?!*' and clicked the *Talk* button pointlessly up and down. I went back into the sitting room, where they were finishing their fish and chips, and said, '*I'm afraid the party's over.*'

Suddenly, we were very sober.

*

When someone says, '*My whole life had been leading up to this moment*,' they're usually talking about something good. But it was true of this too. I had never felt really Grown-up. Now it was as though a lid had been lifted. I felt a rush of power charge through me. There was a feeling of facing a tidal wave, but also of riding the top of it, of drowning and surfing at the same time.

St Thomas's Hospital had the builders in, giving it an air of 1970s unfinished Spanish hotel. We had to step over a man digging up the corridor. In my head I could hear Dad saying: '*You'd think they'd at least finish the place before letting out rooms.*'

The most trivial things came into sharp focus. Every comment, look or touch was exaggerated, the colour and sound turned way up. Debby was in a room which was carpeted but for some reason had a shower head sticking out of the wall. Maybe the seismic effect of his death had warped the entire physical world, so that nothing would be quite normal ever again. Perhaps showers in rooms with carpets was just the beginning. Soon there'd be baths on buses or trees with taps.

Dad was in another room. Claire said we should go and look at him, which I would never have dared do alone. I was terrified of seeing a dead person, and, absurd as it might sound, scared that he might wake up and be angry with us for letting him end up there. I didn't think he could actually be *Dead*. We crept in. He looked the same, but so very still. He was under a sheet, in a white gown with a frilled neck, which gave him the appearance of a middle-aged choirboy, albeit a Jewish one. One hand was outside the sheet, the other in. Whoever'd laid him out wasn't into symmetry.

Claire said, '*We can touch his hand – it's OK.*' And I wondered how she knew what to do. We said goodbye, but it seemed cruel just going off without him. I didn't want to leave him there on his own.

We stepped back over the man digging the corridor and were given the brown envelope containing the things he had on him when he died: his glasses, his watch, £2.57 in change and his wallet containing the cinema ticket, a 15p stamp, two £10 notes, his Travel-card, and the home-made tag from a Christmas present I'd given him where I'd spaced the lettering badly and had to put 'Christ-mas' on two lines. There was also an information sheet with the number of a bereavement counselling service. This was much worse than seeing his body. Suddenly I felt the life ebb out of me, as if I was just a shell. Debby went home to her children, and we three went back and sat in my bed.

*

'We have to ring Mum.'

She and Dad were divorced almost thirty years ago, but were pretty close. Once they didn't have to be married to each other, they got on fine. She'd provided moral support after his first heart attack, the one the doctor called an 'episode'.

'Yeah, but it's one o'clock. There are no trains. If we wake her now, she'll just be left on her own with the – shock, and—'

'OK,' I said. 'I'll do Mum, you can do Pat.'

Pat was Dad's right-hand person at work, and friend. She might take it even worse than Mum.

'I'll ring her at 7.30. Then she can be on a train by nine.'

We thought about previous Life Events.

'D'you remember when I pushed a bead up my nose and went to hospital to have it tweezed out?'

'How could I? I wasn't born.'

'There were all these doctors looking down at me. About five of them, just for a bead up my nose.'

'No wonder the NHS is in trouble. D'you remember when I tripped over a loose paving stone and Mum fell on top of me?'

'Oh my God . . . !'

We laughed. Peter stirred and muttered: 'Can you

34

keep it down a bit? I'm trying to get some sleep.' And we giggled again.

When we were little, if we'd had a bad dream and came into Mum's room, she would spring to attention instantly with her parent's sixth sense. I thought: *This is the most important thing I am ever going to say to her.*

'Hello, Mum. Mummy. It's Steff.'

I could just tell that she knew. I never ring her at 7.30 for a start.

'It was his heart, wasn't it? Of course,' she said flatly. 'Of course.'

The Coroner's office said there was likely to be a post-mortem, since 62-year-olds aren't supposed to drop dead in the middle of Al Pacino films. There was a chance that the GP could issue the death certificate without a post-mortem, but only if he'd seen him within the last ten days, and anyhow, the receptionist wasn't terribly co-operative.

'Could you tell him that he's died, please?', I said. But all she would say was, 'I can't give out the doctor's number!' the pitch of her voice rising each time. Her tone suggested I might somehow compel her to do it – possibly by witchcraft.

'I don't want his number,' I said. 'Can you just *tell* him? Tell him he has died.' She wouldn't. I knew they occasionally had lunch together, so his home number was likely to be in his book. But he tended to list people under idiosyncratic headings – *'Nice Hedge Man'*, for example, and I couldn't find the doctor under *'Doctor'*, *'Nice Doctor'* or even his name.

I could hear myself sounding calm, which was bizarre, considering I lose my temper, just like him, over far smaller things. My anger at the receptionist gave me a vanishing point, a plughole down which to direct my outrage at this catastrophe.

The registrar was an attractive young black woman in a turban. Dad would have flirted with her, but she would have handled it, I could see that. Having dealt with people in every possible condition of despair and elation, she wasn't fazed by our questions at all.

'This must be an interesting job,' I said.

'Yes, it is,' she conceded. 'Especially when couples come in separately to register a baby.'

'Really? How d'you mean?' This was good; Peter and I were now chatting to someone about her job, not establishing that my father was Dead.

'Mmm. Sometimes there's a fight over its name.'

'What, actual fighting? In here?'

'Oh yes.'

Her machine had finished printing. She read patiently over the details, printed out the certificate and signed her name. I wonder if she feels proud, having her name on the most important piece of paper most of us will ever own, thousands of them, in drawers and filing cabinets all over the city.

The will said: *'I wish to be buried with my mother and sister at Walton Abbey, Herts.'*

'He's misspelled Waltham Abbey! Or whoever typed it has.'

'Oh, for God's sake!'

'Er, hang on. Isn't it United Synagogue?'

'So?'

'They're Orthodox. He's not a member.'

'Oh, bloody hell! What are we supposed to do now?'

'And you say he was Jewish. Can you prove that?' said the woman from the United Synagogue.

Of course he was Jewish. He didn't have a toolbox and constantly gave unsolicited advice. How many people d'you get in here, pretending to be Jewish after they're dead?

'Er . . . well. I'm not quite—'

'Have you got his *talit* and *t'filin?*'

His *what?*

'Er – I haven't found it yet. Them. Yet.'

This, I learned afterwards, was the box with his fragment of the Torah from his bar mitzvah, which I didn't find, and his *kappel* and prayer shawl, which I did, much later, still in their special, embroidered bag.

'His mother's buried at Waltham Abbey?'

'Yes. And his sister and aunt.'

'Have you got the grid reference?'

Grid reference . . .?

Eventually, after some searching, I found a little card that said: *Row M, Section WA*. That did the trick. That, and a cheque for £2,400.

For £2,400, personally I think you should get a Welcome Pack, but anyhow. What you're allowed to say in an Orthodox service is very limited, and only the Rabbi can say it, so it had to be formal and brief. I scribbled a eulogy in the taxi driven by my ex-boyfriend Ian, who'd been close to Dad. It sounded like a reporting exercise he might have given me as a joke: *'Write 150 words on a person you know well, in thirty minutes, in a moving vehicle.'*

Peter said, 'I can't believe you're doing this.'

But this wasn't the hard bit.

The Rabbi wore green wellies evocative of non-Jewish, country pursuits. He had no time for us amateur Jews with our non-qualifying mother and lack of basic procedural knowledge. We were ushered into a gloomy hall with no candles, no flowers nor decorations of any kind. Nor was it heated. The men stood in a line along one wall, the women along the other, like participants in some kind of joyless dance, perhaps an Amish wedding. The coffin lay on a two-wheeled trailer, like a gun carriage, covered with a black cloth. After the eulogy we filed out behind it to an almost totally white exterior. It had snowed and the only contrast was a row of black, leafless trees in the distance. Nearly all the gravestones were white, with the odd rectangle of green marble chips, like swimming pools seen from a plane. And again, no flowers. I could hear Dad saying, '*A well-designed funeral, but it could do with a touch of colour.*' There was – a great big, yellow JCB just yards away from the grave. The lack of decoration is meant to emphasize the spiritual, so I was surprised that all the squeamishness about dahlias didn't extend to diggers.

Led by Stanley, Dad's oldest friend, the men said *Kaddish*. I didn't know, or had forgotten, that custom requires a *minyan* – not *mignon*: that's steak – which means ten Jewish men, in order to say the prayer for the dead. It was long afterwards I realized we had only four at most. Months later, Stanley confessed he had faked it, which made me feel secretly triumphant. *We never even had ten Jewish men, so there.*

I couldn't watch the box going in, couldn't bear the idea of leaving him there. He had never wanted to leave me, and it couldn't be possible he was doing so now. Claire and I looked away, clinging to each other. She said, 'The he that was *him* isn't in there.'

But if he wasn't there, where was he?

We went to his friend Rosemary's house for champagne and cake. I thanked everyone for coming and told one of his favourite jokes, which he'd once sent me in a letter:

'A blind beggar holds out his hand for alms, and a passer-by gives him a matzo.* He grabs the matzo, feels it all over and says: "*Who wrote this shit?!*" '

Who indeed.

Peter said, 'You did that very well.'

But apart from the matzo joke, I couldn't remember a word I'd said.

The grief you might be expecting; no one tells you about the admin.

* A kind of large, square cracker.

While everyone else was crying and Emotionally Processing, grieving, Claire and I did paperwork. Oh, so *this* is being a Grown-up: not losing your father, filling out forms. Every few days I had minutely detailed chats with Alan, the accountant, and came off the phone ready to impress Peter with my new vocabulary. If the phone rang and by any chance it wasn't Alan, I dropped mention of my duties casually into every conversation.

'Hi, how are you? Not too bad. Yes, it is a dreadful shock. I'm just doing the Chargeable and Non-Chargeable Assets. I thought there might be some Potentially Exempt Transfers, but apparently not.'

If I'd had a willy, it would definitely have stiffened. On the one hand, I quite enjoyed signing letters: *S & C Calman, Executors.* On the other hand, it was like the ultimate school detention.

'So *boring*, all this paperwork,' said our mother and Debby.

Personally I didn't find it at all boring, handing over nearly half my inheritance to the last people Dad wanted to have it. Nor were we bored when we found our solicitor hadn't sent in the forms. With the added complication of the business to wind up, and a half-completed tax return – do try not to die in the middle of doing your tax return – it took ten months.

Stick that in your slide rule, whoever failed me at O level maths.

There was an upside. Being furious with the vultures at the Treasury felt better than the hollow, winded feeling of loss. And there were a few juicily satisfying moments, such as getting BT to cancel a posthumous phone bill.

'Are you saying,' I snapped finally, 'that my father used the phone *after he died*??!'

'Er, no,' said the man on the other end.

God, I was powerful. If I could get BT to cancel a bill, I could do anything. When Claire later remembered that we had in fact made a few calls from his place while selling it, my triumph was complete.

After selling the house and business and gathering the letters of condolence into a decently fat folder, I saw myself growing into a kind of benign, female Don Corleone, dispensing favours to grateful friends and business associates from behind a table at my father's favourite tea shop. *You're the Head of the Family now*, I whispered to myself in hoarse, Brandoesque tones. The nearest I got was helping Claire hold a lunch party at the house, her idea for a nice way to give our friends some of the excess furniture. Carrying chairs and tables over a bumpy, mole-holed lawn didn't quite match the splendour of Coppola's wedding scene, but seeing as none of us was carrying a gun, the atmosphere was considerably more relaxed. And there was nobody screwing in the bathroom – at least, nobody who's owned up.

Some time after, something came back to me that the man in my local fax shop had said. When it happened to him, he observed, 'When your father dies, you move up one, don't you? It's like you're next.'

It made me think of those games they used to have in amusement arcades, where there'd be a line of pennies moving towards the edge of a kind of shelf, and the idea was to try and catch them. But they moved very slowly. That's how we are, I suppose, all inching towards the edge.

Father's Day came. I was with Peter in Fenwicks, heading for the café, which was next door to the gift department. Every surface was laden with soap golf balls and so on. Seeing the word *Father* all over the place I burst into tears, and at that moment all the lights went out. It was a power cut, but strangely gratifying, as if the universe had recognized the enormity of my loss.

I was definitely now a Grown-up. So why didn't it last?

5 Fridge Magnates:
Why Mothers Remember *Everything*
and Fathers Don't Have To

My mother always used to say that the one thing you could be sure of when you had children was that you'd have to Grow Up. She wasn't saying it in a 'be warned', finger-wagging sort of way, just observing that it put you in a position where the nature of the role demanded that you face up to certain *responsibilities*. By the sound of it, you didn't have to worry about it in advance; the sheer fact of having children just made it happen.

Unfortunately, in my case, it hasn't.

I'm all right with the structural things: sorting out clean uniform, feeding the kids proper meals, making them brush their teeth and go to bed. I'm even quite good on appearances, e.g. making sure Lydia goes out with neat hair – or at least I was, before she began to treat having a ponytail as an enfringement of her human rights. But the more *conceptual* stuff, such as – well, having the right *attitude*, defeats me. And as for Consistency, it's like Fooling the People; I guess we can all achieve it some of the time.

That simple little instruction from Billy's dad in the park, *Be the Grown-up*, is definitely – with the possible exception of 'Put that wine away for later' – the least attainable goal I've ever been set. When I tell my friend Mark, thinking he'll go, *'Oh, me too,'* he says: 'But you have to be the Grown-up. You can't be the child, because they are.'

Oh, *really* . . . .?

We wake up and although it's early, incredibly early (when was the last time we had a lie-in?), there's always this terrible *rush*. One minute it's 6.30 or whatever, and there's bags of time. Then suddenly it's 7.45! Quarter to eight, for God's sake, and nobody's ready. The kids are getting the cornflakes out and saying, *'There's no toy in this cereal,'* and *'We don't like these,'* and we're saying, *'Well, these are what we've got,'* thinking, *Ungrateful little buggers* – I can feel myself about to go into the Starving Children in Africa speech but don't, because that's

another of those things that used to annoy me about
the school dinner ladies, one of those things, in fact,
that I promised myself I wouldn't say, though quite
frankly I wouldn't mind a bit of *appreciation* around
here.

Anyhow, I shove the cornflakes in the bowls and the
milk vaguely in as well, and Peter says, *'Have you seen my
blue tie?'* And I say, *'Which blue tie is that?'* And he says,
*'You know, the one I wore yesterday. I need it for the meeting/
presentation/blah/whatever, and I'm going to be late, since you
ask.'* And so I look for the tie, at the same time as
looking for the school bags, Lawrence's spelling words
and Lydia's French Week diary which still isn't finished
and probably never will be finished because we'll still
be doing it when she's forty-five, and while I'm doing
that Lawrence is saying, *'I need my swimming trunks,'* and
I say, *'But swimming's on Friday,'* and he says, *'It IS
Friday, STUPID!'* and I say, *'Don't call me stupid!'* while
thinking, how can I not know what day it is? I used to
know stuff like that. Shit, *Friday* – Sally or Annie or
whatever her name is, will be here in a minute in her
car, which is cleaner and newer than ours, to take them
to school.

Except Lydia can't find her shoes, for which I con-
duct a nationwide search, only by the time I find them
I discover they're completely scuffed and muddy, have

chewing gum on them even, and I think, *I can't send her to school like that, what will all the other mothers think?* Especially the really neat ones, whose children are never late or in the wrong kit. What is it with people like that? How do they do it? Maybe they never have sex. *I* never have sex.

But this train of thought is interrupted by Lawrence getting toothpaste on his clean shirt – and then reacting with outrage when I try to put on a clean one. Lydia's saying, *'We have to bring in something volcanic today.'* 'What?! WHY??!!' *'It's Bring Something Volcanic Day. Oh, I can't find my coat.'* 'Where is it, for God's sake?!' *'How should I know? I lost it!'* and then he says: *'Have you got my note for the class trip to the Drug Rehabilitation Unit? You still haven't given it to me and today's the last day.'* And I think, *Rehabilitation Unit? That sounds good, I think I'll check in.* And Lydia says, *'I can't find my homebook,'* and like an airliner brought down by a missing 0.5 mm panel screw, the whole thing goes into freefall. And even as I'm thinking that, my husband – if I've still got one – is going into Basil Fawlty mode: *'Right! I'll deal with it!'*

And what that really means is: *You haven't even kissed me properly for ages.* And I feel old and fat and horrible, and I'm sure he fancies the girl in the deli – having suddenly developed a craving for *artichoke hearts* he never had before, and she's about nineteen and a size 8, so who wouldn't? And the reason Sally or Annie or whoever does the school run on Thursdays hasn't turned up is because it is, indeed, *Friday*, and therefore my turn . . .

And somewhere out there, Sally or Annie or whatever her name is's children are waiting for me to collect them, and I am still here, at home, in a T-shirt that says *Another Shitty Day in Paradise* – hah! – that my friend brought me back from Ibiza, who doesn't have children and still does things like go on holiday in September, go shopping v-e-r-y s-l-o-w-l-y, read more than one paragraph of a newspaper and have the odd facial or massage or something NICE. The post plops onto the mat: something scary-looking from the bank, something demanding we raise money for the school and a letter from the doctor saying my smear test is twenty-five years overdue.

I rush up to the bathroom to look for that old pumice stone I used to use to smooth the bumps on my feet – that's volcanic, isn't it? But it's not there because it's in the Bionicles box – not that I know this. And any minute, Sally or Annie or whatever her bloody name is, will *phone me*. Because *she* knows what day it is, *she* isn't standing there in her T-shirt forgetting to pick up someone else's children, *she* hasn't stumbled downstairs without a note for the school trip and failed to find her husband's blue tie who she hasn't kissed for ages – she . . .

And Sally or Annie or whatever her name is, armpits stubbly, legs unwaxed, half a cup of cold coffee on the windowsill next to the unwatered box tree that cost an absolute fortune and is practically dead, is halfway out with her children to her messy, unattractive car that smells of the cheese triangle one of them left in the footwell, feeling like shit because it's four months since she even kissed her husband properly – and they've just had a row – when she suddenly thinks, *Shit! It's not my day at all!'*

In more ways than one.

Do women make better Grown-up Parents than men? I don't know, but they certainly try very hard. If you opened the average maternal brain you would see, on its neural pathways, millions of tiny bobbles like a blizzard of synaptic Post-it Notes. Even the Brain of a Single Female contains a hell of a lot of things: bras, buns, books, shoes, career ladders, flat conversions, sex, vodka, money, travel, the Reproduction Question and why those Gü chocolate mousses have to be quite so incredibly small. But the Maternal Brain contains 100 times as much thought as that. It is quite literally stuffed. And no one has been able to explain the scientific process by which it manages to absorb more information all the time without blowing up.

Men don't have as many of these bobbles. It's not because they are 'simple mammals', as Peter likes to put it – generally when he's trying to get out of doing some task. It's because they don't have to. They don't need to have their minds cluttered up with the whereabouts of swimming kits or a model of Jupiter for Planets Topic, remembering to run up a costume of a famous character for Book Week, the date of Read With Your Parent Day, Bake with the Class Day, the meeting to Prepare for French Week and Inset Day – otherwise known as Put Your Head In the Oven Day – or football, or ballet, which day they need £2 to go to the National Gallery so they can buy a Monet's *Water-lilies* pencil that falls behind the radiator never to be seen again, who in 4P to invite for a play date to help them devastate their bedroom, and who *not* to invite, and what number tooth they've just lost so the Tooth Fairy can congratulate them in her correspondence, to be sent in a tiny envelope made at midnight out of the edge of an old school letter warning about nits.

Why? Because women generally do all this stuff.

*

Even without the ravages wreaked by parenting, the brains of the two genders show certain differences. You don't even have to dissect them; you can tell by their owners' choice of reading matter.

Take newspapers. I don't know any male who reads the pages called *Things* – or *Gosh!* or *Fluff* – subliminally marked *'Girly Bits about Emoting & Sofa Covers – Please Discard'*. In fact, the reason they're all in a separate section is precisely so that men, whose time is so *valuable*, can easily throw them away. And for those who are too busy even to read a whole title they're often just called '2', so they can be removed from the main section painlessly, and not glanced at even by mistake. Soon, when everything is microchipped, newsagents' shelves will be able to detect a Y chromosome approaching and assemble the paper accordingly. No relationships, dyslexia, bed-wetting, infidelity, Ten Best Lampshades or diets. Not for nothing is news called 'hard', and features 'soft'. But men *can* do soft, if they want to.

One night, way back, I was talking to Ian, the father of a boy in Lawrence's class who'd been trying a new technique with his son. He told me, 'Instead of saying, "William, put your shoes on!" I say, "I'd like you to put your shoes on, please, William." And it works.'

Where did he get this from? I had to know.

'Oh, I read about it in *The Times*.'

You see? He bravely opened the *T2* section, took a deep breath and just stepped in.

That's because much of what's believed about the male and female brains is bollocks. Peter and I did a quiz once, which was supposed to highlight these differences and show how they manifest themselves in everyday life. The question I remember best was: *'If you're doing the ironing with the radio on and the phone rings, do you have to put the iron down and turn off the radio before you can talk?'* After listening to his hilarious chuckle at the thought of my doing the ironing, we put 'No' for me, and 'Yes' for him, and carried on down the list.

But the predicted result of the quiz failed to be achieved when I diverged from the spatially challenged female stereotype because I do know where north is, and can actually read maps. Meanwhile Peter found that he had been able, on occasion, to do more than one thing at once. The result, according to the quiz, was that I'm gay and he's a woman. It evidently couldn't cope with the idea that my husband is in touch with his feminine side, while I have so-called 'masculine' qualities such as the ability to get across London without ending up in Kent. In other words, no-one is 100 per cent anything.

Except when it comes to The Fridge.

*

Recently, for reasons that needn't detain us here, Peter's employment pattern started changing, away from a fully employed kind of scenario, towards a more-occasionally-employed kind of thing. And I've been getting, well, busier. So some while back we sat down like two very adult adults, and decided to redistribute – slightly – the burden of parental responsibility. He very generously offered to do the school run two days a week – there are five school days in the week so obviously it can't be *completely* fair – although actually he ended up doing it four days. So I agreed to let him have one night off completely which was the least I could do since he also puts them to bed pretty much every night while I make the dinner (see Chapter 6: Five Portions of Guilt). So we sorted that out, and had some more wine, and thought how very mature and fair we were. And then I brought up the Rest of It.

And he said: 'The Rest of It?'

Every single woman I've spoken to, without exception – and before I can even get to the end of the question – can list 100 things to do with looking after a house and children that their husbands/partners/whoever completely ignore. And what's more, their husbands/partners/whoever quite often agree. They do ignore them.

One reason for this is because we always do them. For example, I had a friend years ago whose parents offered her a dishwasher, but her boyfriend said they didn't need one, on the grounds that there was *'hardly any washing-up to do'*. And as she explained to him, 'There's hardly any washing-up to do because I ALWAYS DO IT.' Thus it fell into the Black Hole wherein all things are rendered Invisible. Other contents of the Black Hole include:

- Picking clothes up off the floor
- Carrying things up which have been left on the stairs
- Putting clothes into the dirty washing box
- Unloading washing machine
- Hanging up clothes
- Ironing
- Setting the table
- Folding things
- Putting crisp bags in the bin
- Digging the remains of Babybels, Starbursts, uneaten apples, etc. out of the recesses in the doors of the car
- Excavating the furry cheese, yogurt miasmas and jugs of live gravy from the back of the fridge
- Washing the dishes

- Wiping the draining board
- Emptying out the cider-y apple slices and ancient sandwiches from the bins in the children's rooms which you installed to inspire them to be tidy, and which they have only ever used once
- Cleaning the bath
- Cleaning the loo
- Taking homework/letters/wet swimming things/ smelly games kit out of school bags
- Putting homework/letters/dry swimming things/ fragrant games kit into school bags
  And:
- Making any arrangements for the children, in or out of school

Peter would like me to point out that he *personally* does quite a lot of these things, but I'll come to that later. It is my book, after all.

There are two, or maybe three, reasons for this rather considerable blindspot. First, husbands/fathers/ people of the male persuasion have been allowed to believe that skills are primarily gender-based. And yes, some of them are. The ability to pee in a pub car park, just feet away from a perfectly good lavatory, is something men are usually better at. And managing to spend an hour saying goodbye to someone they've just spent the evening with is where women generally seem to have the edge. But not *all* skills are divided up this way. It is *not*, for example, the prerogative of women to be able to answer the phone.

Peter, for instance, *can* answer the phone, but doesn't *like* to because it might be about *arrangements*. And arrangements is one of the things he Doesn't Do. So picture the scene at BMC HQ, when the phone rings and – by some oversight – he picks it up.

'Oh, are you? Ha-ha! You'd better speak to my Wife!'

'Why? Who's that?'

'The Browns. They want to know if lunch is still on next Sunday.'

'So why can't you deal with it? I'm cooking' (see Chapter 6: Five Portions of Guilt).

'I don't know what you've got planned.' And he backs away, flapping his hands as if avoiding something contagious.

So I have the conversation, chop the carrot sticks, co-ordinate the chicken, potatoes and green whatevers that won't get eaten, *and* check the calendar, while he behaves like someone who not only doesn't know the people in question, he doesn't even *live* here.

This is how he's able to keep his mind so clear and sparkling fresh. And why he displays a certain impatience when I don't snap to it and remember some arcane bit of information about an old friend of his whom I met for four seconds at a wedding fourteen years ago:

'You know – he was in Miss Trubshaw's class with me at Ecclesall Infants. He had a toy bus conductor's set.'

It's no good saying: 'You don't seem to realize my mind is stuffed. I've had to absorb 1,400 thoughts since teatime. I can't get any more in; it's like a bulging suitcase as it is. Any more and it'll explode into a million pieces and make a mess on the carpet – which no one will clear up, except me, except I won't be able to because my brain will be all over the carpet. Forget it, just Forget It.' Because he just doesn't have any idea.

He will come into the kitchen, gaze despondently at the patchwork of paper that covers the fridge, then look at the newspapers, school letters, menus, kids' drawings, CDs, etc. on the worktop and say – as if he's driving down a pleasant country road which has become blocked:

'Any chance we could clear some of these PILES?'

And I'll say: 'Sure, if you want to just chuck away all our essential information. I mean, it's all – you know, to do with the house, local stuff and bloody *school*.'

Yes, these are not 'MY' piles They are Family Piles.

There are also School Piles, Community Piles and National Piles. (The *International* Piles are his.) He then manages to pick out the *one thing* amongst them which isn't.

'What's this?'

'A catalogue of Italian vegetable seeds which I thought I might plant. When we get the garden sorted out.'

'And *this*?'

OK, two things.

'A letter from my old headmaster.'

He puts them down again, shaking his head.

'Well, YOU could deal with some of it.'

'I mean, it's just so – you know.'

'So *you* go through it then.'

There is a PAUSE.

'Look, I'll put it all in your study and you can sort it out later.' 'Later'? What 'later'?! Like he's doing me some kind of favour. I don't have a 'later'. He then passes the fridge and stops, like a UN Inspector survey- ing the aftermath of something. 'I mean, you just can't *see* anything.'

I never did neurology, though I'm pretty sure I could fit it in between the school run and dinner if I felt the urge. But I reckon it's quite possible that the male brain contains a tiny satellite dish which scrambles those vital pieces of information and sends a signal to their retinas that converts them into meaningless scribbles.

And anyhow, he cannot take up his precious brain with any of these things because he has More Important Things on his mind: 'Darling, I think you should read this piece about how men don't like discussing relationships.'

'Mmm, in a minute.'

'It's all about how they feel threatened so they use avoidance tactics.'

'Yeah? Put it over there and I'll read it later.'

Ha-ha, and if you think that's bad enough, he said *this* to me once: 'Why don't *you* read it, and tell me what it says?'

The far more important thing he was reading at the time? A biography of Sir Alec Issigonis, creator of the Mini. I only mention this because I have the highest respect for the man and his cars, and do not *in any way* seek to suggest that my husband's reading matter is pointless. Besides, I bought it for him. It's just the *hierarchy* I object to.

However, we can't blame men for thinking their time is more valuable than ours, because we've brought it on ourselves by spending so much of it with our noses buried in various sorts of unnecessary advice. And it's not just a few newspaper pages on a Sunday, is it? We buy millions of magazines full of it – not to mention stacks of books with titles like, '*Why Men Don't Listen & Women – Oh, Just Give Us £14.99.*'

It's not just complicated things, like parenting and plumbing; those we all need help with. Women are continually seeking guidance on *everything*: How to Look Slimmer, Be Thinner, Seem Taller, Come Over as Less of a Chub; How to Get a Raise, Sound More Confident, Buy a New Car in Lichtenstein & Make Christmas Table Centrepieces from Old Bits of Cork; How to Teach Your Child Particle Physics at Home; How to Restore an Entire Stately Home With Just a Trestle Table & a Jolly Super Attitude – I'm not exaggerating: that one was in the *Daily Telegraph* – and 'How To Get On In Life But Make Everyone Like You & Nobody Hate You Ever Ever Ever'. So we're constantly undermining our own confidence.

He can't remember anything to do with the children apparently, because he has More Important Things on his Mind. Or did I just tell you that? Yes, well, I know no one's ever listening to me, so I might as well say everything twice.

Some of the Important Things my husband has on His Mind:

- Is this jumper getting too saggy?
- Should I get a new one?
- Did I wash my hair this morning?
- Should I have a pooh now or wait until after the news?

But in order to make things *fair*, and because he has now started reading over my shoulder to check, I *will* now concede that he *personally* does quite a lot of the things on the list you read earlier.

Indeed, one of the reasons I became fond of him in the first place was that he turned up for our first holiday together with a travel iron. And no, he did not hand it to me on the first night with his shirts. Of course, he later balanced this out with loads of fantastically annoying habits and deficiencies that would not only cancel out the ironing but make staying married quite a challenge. But at the time, I thought I'd found the Holy Grail. Funny, isn't it? My dream man was big with a hairy chest and could cook, and I wound up with someone quite thin with less hair on his chest than I have, who hates cooking. Yes, yes, and who *will do the ironing*. As with children, you don't get what you dreamed of. You get something different, maybe better, but also annoying in a thousand ways you never imagined.

Anyway, as I said, we've been redistributing the parental load. So he has begun to do more of the childcare. He bustles about dispensing squash and supervising homework. And suddenly the household, which has always stumbled from one crisis to another, is a well-oiled machine. This is because he has been doing One Thing.

And just as there are women who think that the calorie clock stops if they eat food without putting it on a plate, and some kids believe you can't get pregnant if you do it standing up, Peter previously thought that while you're looking after children, everything else – just stops. The phone doesn't need answering, toys don't need picking up, clothes don't need to go into the dirty washing box and school letters don't need to be read. Hell, they don't even need to be taken out of the bags. If I came in and said, 'Hello! Did you sign Lydia's permission to go to the theatre?' or whatever, he'd say: 'I've been on child duty, actually,' in a tone of injured incredulity, as if he were a brain surgeon I'd asked to collect my dry cleaning.

Then he started looking after them more often, and witnessed the revelation of an Amazing Truth: while you're looking after children, *other things still need to be done*. I wasn't there at the Actual Moment, but as far as I can tell, he tried moving across to the worktop and signing the permission letter *while* supervising the homework, and found his brain didn't explode. Then, after only a few weeks of that, and a mere seven years after the birth of Lydia, he made them supper. Needless to say, he is Very Pleased.

'It's going really well!' he reports at intervals, puffing up the stairs to my study with a cup of tea.

And that first supper has not been his last. He's been adding to his portfolio, supervising homework, signing permission letters, making supper, tidying the 130,000 bits of felt, coloured paper and half-made Christmas cards in the craft cupboard *and* writing assemblies, swimming galas and so on into his diary. All I have to do is appear at seven, and while he puts them to bed, make our dinner. I love that oasis of time, with a bottle of wine and a CD on, and the brain gradually slipping into neutral. Plus it gets me out of dragging Lawrence and Lydia along that long and winding bedward road, on which they find so many unexpected detours.

It's at times like these I appreciate how truly lucky I am. A couple of years ago I would have felt guilty, coming down to a peacefully empty kitchen, while husband folded school uniforms, read stories and mopped up after their bath. But now I think, *no: that spare capacity in his brain is going to good use. I'll buy him a nice little box of chocs on Father's Day to show I've noticed.*

Ahhh. A sense of enormous satisfaction envelops me at the end of a day's work as I open the fridge to get the wine, but – he's already poured it!

'Here you are, darling.'

'Don't mind if I do. Hang on, what's that wonderful smell?'

He flings open the oven to reveal a roast guinea fowl, plus potatoes, parsnips and leeks, all done to perfection. Then I hear something.

'Where are the children . . .?'

'Just playing on the computer. I let them have an extra fifteen minutes. Cooking's not as hard as I thought,' he announces, flopping down with his wine. 'You don't mind putting them to bed, do you?'

6 Five Portions of Guilt

I have begun to be aware of a discrepancy between our *Idea* of how our children are, and what psychiatrists call *Reality*.

Shakespeare said it is 'a wise man who knows himself to be a fool'. And it's a sensible mother who doesn't change her baby on a £100 antique pink satin quilt. I did actually once see someone do this: it got pooh on it. Similarly, you learn fairly quickly that they're not going to sit pristinely in little white cashmere cardigans with pearl buttons. Because it's only when you have them that you can appreciate, with your entire wretched being, the futility of trying to make them metamorphose into the fairies you've created inside your head – not helped, it must be said, by the magazines. In case you do ever find yourself despairing over your abnormally filthy child – the perfect babies in clean pastel clothes you see in the photos? *The stylists take the dirty clothes off every ten minutes and put on new ones.* Now, there's something to cut out and keep.

Our main delusion in this house is about food. The children I had in my head before I conceived any real ones sat round the table chatting sweetly and eating whatever was put in front of them. I even made the mistake of going to Spain and Italy and seeing it for real, leading me to cling even more determinedly to my dream. But, just as they also manage to live with their in-laws without murdering them, they're obviously aliens whom we will never understand. But it's not fair! As I bark at them to *Eat Up!* and *Stop Kicking Each Other Under the Table!* I just can't conceal my frustration that my children are – well, British. Peter minds less about table manners than me, but he's in full delusional mode when it comes to what they actually consume.

Lydia is invited to tea at a friend's house, and the mother asks me the standard question: 'Is there anything she doesn't eat?'

And I answer breezily: 'Not really! They're pretty eclectic, my lot. They eat stir-fries and curry.'

'*Re-ally?* That *is* good!'

But I am lying, or rather, massaging the truth – OK, rubbing it quite hard – because of brainwashing by their father. This is *his* version. If a policeman took us away and interviewed us separately he would not recognize us as talking about the same family. Peter has this need to spin things to sound very *positive*, as if he's suddenly become an MP.

'How have they been during the holidays?' someone will ask.

'Very good.'

'And what are the evenings like?'

'Great.'

No mention of the fighting, whingeing and currently horrendous battle to get them to stay in bed. Not a peep about the fact that Lawrence, and sometimes Lydia as well, has begun coming down to the kitchen with increasingly implausible justifications for their failure to be asleep:

'I'm hungry.' (Possibly true: he metabolizes food like a heavyweight boxer in training and has to be refuelled constantly, like the boiler on a steam train.)

'Lydia keeps disturbing me.' (Also often true: she's discovered that chatting after lights out winds him up and so has begun to do it much more.)

'I'm too hot.' (This *was* true during the summer, when their room was like a Chinese laundry, but is now straining credulity, due to the drop in temperature at time of writing.)

'My duvet's too heavy.' (Quite frankly I'm starting to lose patience with this one.)

'*I heard a funny noise.*' (Well, yes, quite possibly, but their hearing's so sharp at that age they can hear a squirrel coughing in the woods two miles away, so in order to solve that problem we would have to move to New Zealand.)

Anyhow. About food.

At the hospital breastfeeding workshop before I had Lawrence, we were advised to change our diets.

'You should avoid spicy foods,' admonished the midwife, sounding weirdly like the voice on my computer that intones, '*Alert! The printer cannot be found. But it doesn't matter because what you are writing is rubbish.*' I thought: *Bugger off, mate. Curry is one of my favourite foods.* It was sustaining me through the hot, lumbering third trimester and I wasn't about to give it up.

'Hmm. Where are you from?' I asked her.

'Sri Lanka.'

'So what do they eat in your country when they're breastfeeding?'

'Well, the same as usual.'

'*Ah-ha!*'

There was a brief silence, and then someone asked if it was OK to have 5 mg of caffeine after twenty-four weeks.

Later I attributed my children's liking for interestingly flavoured food to all that chicken jalfrezi coming through the placenta. But what I can't understand is why, as they get older, they're getting *more* fussy, not less.

'*They eat stir-fries and curry.*' Well, ye-es, inasmuch as they eat noodles. And occasionally bean sprouts which I *tell* them are noodles but shorter – though actually they've now rumbled this, and prawns. Prawns they like. No onions, though, peppers, mushrooms, baby sweetcorns or beans. 'Curries' means chicken korma, and lately Lydia has begun to cut up rough about even that. If we have an Indian takeaway, Lawrence – who at least likes tandoori *and* tikka, always keeps everyone else's pots of green or orange sauce and has it, sometimes with bread dipped in it, for breakfast. And while I'm impressed that he's already begun to prepare for life as a student, it's futile, as by the time he's that age any kind of further education will only be achievable with an immense loan which his grandchildren will have to pay back. Lydia meanwhile has begun to eat smaller and smaller particles of chicken tikka, or even shashlik – *which isn't spicy/YES IT IS!/No it ISN'T/YES IT IS!!!* – no longer visible to the naked eye, until she and I stare miserably at each other, she like a hunger-striking suffragette and me a prison warder, and I say:

69

'OK, I'll make you a bowl of pasta.'

I can remember taking them to the canteen at Peter's office, years ago, and giving them *vegetable korma* which they *liked*. Where have those children gone now? I like vegetables. Peter likes them. The children like *some* of them – if you live on one of those Pacific islands where 'some' is the same as 'two'. Basically, it's broccoli and carrots. Carrot *stick*. And even then they often leave those until they're cold when, not surprisingly, they don't taste very nice. And that's when I see the evening disappearing and my life ebbing away, and start barking, 'Eat your broccoli!' I can't stop myself saying it – even when we're not at the table. In the street. I sat next to a woman in a café the other day who left hers. Tch tch, what a waste. And I was just leaning across to say, 'Come on, you've hardly touched it,' when Lydia said, 'Mummy, you don't know that lady!'

I suppose I'll end up being diagnosed with *Florets Syndrome*. Mind you, I knew a woman who once started cutting up someone else's meat at a dinner party.

Still, why should we beat ourselves up about it when we've got the government to do that for us? How many children *do* eat enough veg? If we have to negotiate for half an hour to get them to eat two carrot sticks, how the fuck does the government think we're going to give them five portions a *day*? Who eats five portions of *anything* a day? These bastards just issue these guidelines to make people like me feel inadequate.

'Hey, what can we announce this week to make parents feel like useless shites? I know! Let's tell them their kids have got to have five portions of vegetables a day!'

'What's a portion?'

'Dunno. Who cares? They'll never manage it anyway.'

'Yeah, great! This is even better than when we said they could only have twenty-one units of alcohol!'*

As for fruit, about two months ago, they both *asked for oranges* and *ate them*. In fact, two each. I immediately got on the phone to various people so I could drop it into the conversation: *'How are you?' 'Fine: just giving the children their ORANGES'* – but by the time I'd done that they were running amok round the kitchen and pulling each other along the floor like John Belushi in *Animal House*. We could not get them up to their bath for anything. We puzzled over this for a while, and could only come to the conclusion – extremely reluctantly, of course, that fruit made them hyper.

But it's OK because we've got an excuse. We *would*

---

* An amount that the editor of *The Lancet* later admitted they made up.

have more fruit and vegetables in our diet if we could get them. If anyone from the government is reading this, and the way Blair is going, it's highly likely, it's a supply problem, OK? I prefer to buy them from the greengrocer's and we even have one in the area, which means there's no excuse for getting them from a supermarket. It's not just that supermarkets infuriate me with their patronizing ad campaigns and sanitized environments like giant fridges – although far cleaner than ours. My greengrocer is not only a Human Being as opposed to Greed Incorporated, he lets you choose exactly the lettuce or tiny bit of ginger you want, lets you try the apples *and* sells bread, eggs, rice, porridge, jam and CHOCOLATE. And when you've got more than two bags, he carries them to your car – although that does make me feel a bit old.

So when I *am* in a supermarket, especially en route from work to home, when I don't have the car and can't carry much – but even when I'm not, I can buy anything *except* vegetables because I will get home, get in the car, and go to the greengrocer's. But I don't.

It's not on the way to anywhere, the parking's quite tricky, and I can't stop everything to make a separate trip to buy vegetables because I'm *working*, but if I go after school with the children when it's not my Golden Time, there's no parking on that side of the road after

4 p.m. so it's even worse. And anyway, when we *do* do that they always moan and fight, because they're so tired. The greengrocer does take orders for delivery, but he's got no email, only fax – which we got rid of because the only ones we got were wrong numbers for medical conferences in the middle of the night – so you have to drop your order in, which sort of defeats the point.

But I *can't* get the vegetables – or indeed, the fruit – from a supermarket, not least because of the prices and especially since I read about apples being gassed. My friends say, 'Why don't you join one of those box schemes?' but why would we, when we've got a greengrocer's so nearby?

Incidentally, we have the same thing with fish, since we have one of Britain's half-dozen remaining fishmongers not that far away, but we don't go there much either – although that's more from being useless than any of the reasons with the veg. But lately we've been able to feel much better about that as well since most fish is either endangered or full of toxins, so we're only supposed to eat two portions a decade instead of our own weight every day in salmon.

And as if all those guidelines weren't annoying enough, celebrity chefs are always telling us that children are born without prejudices, and the way to get them interested in food is to cook with them. To encourage this practice, they have themselves photographed in an extremely irritating way, guaranteed to make the rest of us feel inadequate, baking spontaneously with their adoring offspring. They're always grinning away, covered in flour or chopping garlic and Having a Jolly Time. Well, let me tell you what happens when I try to involve my two in cooking. I don't even attempt garlic chopping but go straight to the nursery slopes: biscuits.

First, they fight over who gets to kneel on the stool nearest me – which is ridiculous as I'm not even popular. Then they fight over the mixer. I finally get them to take turns with it, but neither wants to hold it for more than fourteen seconds.

'Actually, Mummy, I'm a bit tired,' they sigh, as if they've just done double shifts for Gordon Ramsay, as opposed to having been staring at the television for the last two hours picking their noses. So I offer to finish the mixture, promising to tell them when it's time to come back and do the cutting out. When I do, they apply themselves to the cutters with great enthusiasm, stopping only to fight over the one out of twenty that they both absolutely *have* to use at that precise second. They then gradually slow down more and more until production grinds virtually to a halt at about one biscuit an hour. By then most of the mixture has disappeared into their mouths, and the shapes going onto the trays are increasingly un-biscuit like.

'This is a Worm!'

'Mummy! Look, look! This is a Ball.'

'How do you like my Tiny Dots?'

So along with the teddies, aeroplanes and stars done as a precaution by me, a strange pile emerges from the oven of balls which are not cooked at all, and microdots which are incinerated. But they are pleased with them. And it only takes five hours.

And that's making something they *like*.

7 Greed v Laziness: the Eternal Struggle

Children are supposed not to be able to say No to sweet things. If you put out a plate of biscuits for guests, they will supposedly eat every one before the adults have even got their coats off. But that's OK, because you expect it. Lack of willpower is regarded as a characteristic of youth that people – theoretically – grow out of. So what happens when you, the so-called adult, don't? And just how ashamed should you be when you realize that when it comes to sugar, your children have far more restraint?

Whenever my sister and I got chocolate as children, we gobbled it up – if not physically prevented – in one go. Anything put aside for Christmas became the object of a protracted stalking campaign, with chairs leaned against shelves to be climbed on as soon as Mum had turned her back or could be distracted by pathetically transparent attempts:

'Mummy, can you go in the other room, please?'

'Why?'

'We just want you to.'

When it came, Christmas was dominated by uncontrolled consumption that began with the large German honey bread hearts with icing on that were hung from the catches on the windows, and finished with chocolate coins and 'smoking sets' – pipe, cigarettes and sugar matches, finished off with a coloured foil ashtray to be sick into at the end. Our parents, evidently prepared to do anything rather than be woken at five in the morning, just seemed to factor it in as part of the Yuletide experience.

I once saw a Gary Larson cartoon that showed a boy in his pyjamas trying to work up the courage to brave the monsters he thought lurked under the stairs, so he could get to the cookie jar in the kitchen. It spoke to me, that drawing, because it drew attention to the suffering endured by people whose laziness is in constant conflict with their greed. I often waste half an evening debating whether to get in the car and drive to a shop for some chocolate. In the end, though, my laziness usually wins – which probably explains why, even when I'm not eating chocolate, I don't lose weight – because I'm not moving around either. As my sister says, at least if you *walk* to get your chocolate, you deserve *some* respect. For me, it's a Serious Problem, and one that really should be classed as a disability. I mean, one of the reasons this book was handed in late was that I had to keep stopping to eat. I don't *mean* to eat all the time. I don't *want* to. I just have no willpower. But I also have no desire for physical exertion either. So what I do is spend the rest of the evening moaning about not having any chocolate, while Peter sits there, murmuring occasionally, 'Mmm, I could just fancy some choccy.'

And if the children have left any lying around, they'll regret it. For a man who in other ways has a completely normal appetite, he displays a worrying lack of self-control around the confectionery of others. He's the one who supposedly likes 'everything in moderation' and was horrified when I ate a Mars Bar after dinner on one of our early dates. Yet the first time I gave him a chocolate car, a Father's Day novelty about eight inches long, he shoved the whole thing down in about one and a half minutes. So that makes two of us. Yet Lawrence and Lydia are always leaving half-eaten bars and packets of sugary this and that, and frequently forget about them completely. The cupboard right now contains two unfinished bags of M&S piggy sweets and a whole tin of mini Haribos, Mint Aeros and miscellaneous chocolate twiddles – all things they begged for in the shop. Is this *normal*? Is a call to a Child

Psychologist on the cards? Possibly, but Peter and I have each committed serious crimes against our children's edible possessions, so I suppose we're the ones who need help.

About three summers ago, we got quite drunk one night and while roaming the house looking for sweet things, stumbled on the remains of the children's Easter eggs under the stairs. They were in a carrier bag hanging from a coat peg, still in their nuclear-proof plastic casings. As it was by then June, I think it's fair to say they'd been forgotten.

And emboldened by having got away with that, we went on to consume, at various times, Smarties, Mint Aeros, Chocolate Buttons, Fry's Peppermint Cream bars, Milky Bars, Maltesers and the contents of many party bags. The trick was not to get caught smelling of it.

'Night night, darling.'

'Mummy? I can smell chocolate.'

'Can you? *That's* odd.'

And the next day: 'I can't find the rest of my *Twirl*.'

'Really? Are you sure? It was there the other day.'

*

We originally started going through the party bags with the genuine motive of weeding out those hard little lollies like bullets, and the sort of extreme density chews we used to sneak off to buy at school, which not only pull out your fillings but dislocate your jaw. It was Peter who first succumbed to his baser instincts. At first I really was saving the children's teeth; it was only when I fell under his influence that I started thieving from innocent youth.

One night, when the children were in bed, he tiptoed to the cupboard and ate the rest of Lydia's chocolate teddy.

'What are you *doing*??!' I was genuinely shocked.

'She'll never eat all this,' he said. And it was huge. She'd been working her way slowly through it for several weeks. Yet in her father's hands it went down amazingly fast, like the *Titanic*.

'The ears were a particularly satisfying shape,' he said afterwards. And this from a man who once picked on me for taking too much *salad*.

But the next day, consumed with remorse, he decided to confess. Lydia was appalled.

'Well, she's found out what her beloved daddy is really like. She'll probably never get over it,' I said, relishing a rare chance to be the Good One.

It's funny; we'd managed to avoid the Father

Christmas dilemma, only to have to deal with *this*. Guilt drove Peter to Sergio's deli, where he bought her a chocolate rabbit the size of a car.

'So d'you feel you've learned your lesson?' I asked him.

'Yeah. It's best to eat stuff before they get it in the first place.'

I took him at his word.

One Sunday night, Lawrence develops a terrible pain in his lower left side. It gets worse when we touch it, and Peter – who had an appendicitis as a child, thinks he knows what it might be. At the emergency surgery, the doctor concurs with our diagnosis, and we end up in the A&E department of our local hospital. Ex-nanny and chief babysitter Katarina agrees to take Lydia for the night and, if necessary, deliver her to school the next morning, while we take it in turns to look after Lawrence. I am not looking forward to it; the last time we were here, it was so bad we came home.

Over the next three days, various medics attempt to establish whether or not Lawrence's appendix should come out. Since the pain is coming and going, they're not sure. But because they're not sure, from the end of the first night, they stop him from eating anything so if they do have to whip it out, his stomach will be empty. This drags on, with me doing the first night, Peter the second, and me the third. Lawrence and I pass the time in a reasonable frame of mind by reading comics, watching TV, playing 'Squiggles' (one of you draws a squiggle and the other makes it into a picture), wheeling the drip to the loo and back, and testing each other with the interactive science games provided by the hospital's education service. By the time we get to day three, though, he is seriously desperate for some food. The drip has stopped him from actually starving, but his lost appetite – another symptom of appendicitis – has come back. I beg the surgeons to make a decision, but they say they can't yet. They want him to have a scan – a good idea, since if the appendix is enlarged it will tell us.

'We'll soon know one way or the other,' I inform Lawrence confidently.

So we wait ninety minutes in the Ultrasound department, along with people who look as though they've been there all their lives: the very old, the toothless, the malnourished and the hugely fat. On the scan the appendix looks normal but it still hurts. He's still not allowed to eat. It's about 5 p.m. They decide to keep him Nil by Mouth until morning. If he's not in screaming agony by then, he can eat and go home.

'Please decide as soon as you can in the morning,' I beg them. 'Promise?'

As it happens, I haven't eaten anything since a piece of toast for breakfast. Although hungry, I regard my position as one of solidarity with my child; if he can't eat, nor will I. Then the speccy man turns up.

This is a huge, inner-city hospital teeming with the people of a world apart: the black, white and beige denizens of the local estates, the poor, depressed, twitching and drugged, most of them legally. The old ones are thin and crumpled, the younger, plaited and pierced. But Speccy Man is another breed; he carries a diabetic toddler whom he settles into the next door bed, and wears corduroy trousers worn too high on the waist. He looks at me, and I at him.

'Would you like a bit of my *Guardian?*' I offer, in the internationally recognized middle-class gesture of welcome. He accepts. And at about 8.30, when I'm beginning to think I really could go outside and kill a dog, he says, 'I'm popping out to the Portuguese place for fried chicken in a bit. Would you like some?'

I look at Lawrence, feebly turning the pages of his comic, and search my conscience. After about 2.5 seconds I reply, 'Yes, please, yes. But for God's sake don't rustle the bag.'

'Would you like spicy, or lemon and herb?'

'Spicy, but be discreet. Bring it to the end of the ward and leave it on the toy table.'

We exchange a nod. I know there may be worse things done by parents; I know that more insidious substances almost certainly change hands in and around this building every night. And I know also that I am doomed. I will be cast into Parent Hell for this, consigned to an eternity of freezing rugby pitches and 'The Wheels on the Bus'. But I cannot help myself. I am weak, dammit, weak!

So that he won't notice when the chicken arrives, I decide to bore Lawrence to sleep with the dullest reading matter available. His toddler asleep, Speccy Man sets off for the lifts. The clock is ticking. I grab my *Guardian*.

'Tony Blair met EU officials in Brussels yesterday for the first in a series of meetings to—'

Lawrence sits bolt upright.

'This is BORING! I want *Captain Underpants*.' But *Captain Underpants* is far too much fun.

'I can't find it,' I lie. 'How about a nice Greek myth?'

After a bit of persuasion he agrees, and gets back under the covers. The Greeks told a ripping story, so it's a bit of a challenge. The nearest I can come to soporific is the very start of *Jason and the Argonauts*.

'And so Jason came to build the strongest, fairest ship ever seen upon the seas . . .' I lower my voice to little more than

a whisper, and flatten it into a monotone. In a few minutes, he's off.

I put the book away and slip back into my chair. I have a beer which Peter has smuggled in for me, which is stored in readiness in my bag. Ah, that'll be Complete Heaven. I can't wait. I can almost taste the—

NEENAANEENAANEENAA!!!

The bloody toddler's alarm has gone off and she's sitting up, crying.

'DADDEEDADDEEDADDEE!!!'

'Sssh!' I plead. 'Sssh!' But it's no good. She's wet the bed. Lawrence is awake as well.

'What is it?!'

'It's all right, darling. Just the little girl next door. Go back to sleep.'

'I can smell chicken . . .'

'What? No, no, I don't think so . . .'

But sure enough, Speccy Man is coming up the aisle. Like a captured mule at Customs, I wave frantically at him to keep going, but – distracted, I suppose, by the screaming toddler – he dumps the chicken right on our table.

'Chicken . . .' murmurs Lawrence.

'No, no – it's for that little girl's dad. See?'

I turn round and firmly ignore the aromatic bundle

while I continue with *Jason and the Argonauts*. But it takes far longer than before. By the time he is breathing steadily with eyes closed, the meal is cold. But I don't care. I gobble it obscenely, grateful at least that floppy chips don't crackle, and dispose of every scrap of evidence, even burying the paper napkins right down the bottom of the bin. I feel as I imagine a married person feels when they have just slept with someone new, the guilty mind mingling with the sated body to create an entirely new state of being. I am lost, but at least my son still believes in me. I wonder: *How long till the ward round?* By the time he finally does get to eat again, at ten, Lawrence will have been starved for thirty-eight hours.

At 8 a.m. he sits up and looks at me.

'So,' he says. 'How was the chicken?'

8 Go Placidly Amid the Blah

Some years ago I read a piece in the *Guardian* by a woman who lamented the failure of her efforts to persuade her son to play with dolls. It really, really bothered her. And she's not the only one. Every now and then some well-meaning, hand-wringing, over-educated parent – male or female – tries to train the maleness out of their perfectly normal son. And you do have to ask yourself why. Well OK, you don't – unless you're in the habit of arguing with the newspaper and muttering at the television and radio like me. Not all boys are equally keen on guns – Lawrence never has been – but if they do pick up a stick, point it at you and shout *'Bang!'* the least you can do is play dead.

Of course, a boy whose father comes running in with a ceremonial Japanese disembowelling sword shouting, *'Get out of that highchair – it's time to be a Man!'* may experience Inner Conflict later in life. But since the majority of boys do appear to be more physically expressive than girls, why don't we just get on with it? As my sister-in-law observed, after thirty years in education: *'Boys do fight.'* And when I look at Lawrence's schoolmates, they pretty much run the gamut from kids who tend to play too rough and stand like boards with their arms by their sides if you hug them – or rather, if *Lawrence* hugs them – to those who, like him, are affectionate and demonstrative but not 'girlish'. What most of them have in common, though, is fathers who have a fairly fixed idea of how they think they should be.

So my question is this:

Does being a Grown-up *Parent* involve taking charge of those things we *can* influence about our children, and leaving alone those we *can't*? Or, as the poster puts it, should we: *Have the courage to change those things you can, the something to accept those you can't and the wisdom to know the difference*, a piece of advice you can just tell wasn't written by a woman. Like that other saying people used to have on their walls, *Go placidly amid the blah* and all that, it's clearly the product of an uncluttered male brain cloistered for a lot of years with several other uncluttered male brains, unchallenged by love, children, running a car, or any of those features of life that make it impossible and, also, worth living. A mother trying to get that down would get as far as '*Go pla—*' and then have to stop and wipe someone's bottom.

On the one hand, most boys need to run about and hurl themselves at each other quite a bit. On the other, people with very naughty male children, who say adoringly, 'Boys will be boys!' as their son straps a firework to the cat, might want to consider that testosterone is like hydrogen: very useful – and indeed essential to life – but it does need to be *blended*. It's a case of: *Have the wisdom to know the difference between harmless stick play and your child turning into a mini Afghan warlord.*

So, what can – or should we – change, and what not?

One afternoon I am in the kitchen, giving the worktops their weekly wipe. It's quite satisfying, I reflect, that when you wipe something it stays wiped. Well, not forever, but at least no one can dispute that you did wipe it, unlike with parenting, where if you put a child to bed and they get out again, it's as if you never existed at all. Anyhow, there I am wiping, when I hear – instead of the usual rows going on in the next room – chortling. And what's more, it's joint chortling. The children are Doing Something Together.

They're playing a computer game! This is wonderful! Their tinkling laughter fills the room.

'What're you playing, kids?'

'Snowboarding!'

'What site?'

'CBBC.'

'That's lovely!'

Then I hear this: 'Die! Die!'

Or maybe it's *'Dye! Dye!'* and they've switched to a weaving site. Lydia has started a craft class recently, and she's very keen on—

'Ha-ha-ha! Do it again!'

I go in.

'Why are you saying 'Die'?'

'Look!'

'Aren't you meant to go *round* the people?'

'It's more fun this way.'

And as I muse on this over the weekend, I decide it all fits in perfectly with my little-bit-of-testosterone never-did-anyone-any-harm policy of accepting that children do have violent imaginations, and repressing those natural instincts can only lead to trouble later in life. After all, Sigmund Freud said—

'Sticks! They're playing with bloody sticks! Oh, God . . .'

I hate the bloody things. For about the last four years, i.e. half his lifetime, Lawrence has had a mania for them, and he hasn't had a single friend to play who hasn't been equally fascinated. You put them in the garden, the sticks having been hidden from the last time I snatched them off him, and within 4.5 seconds they're fencing; long, pointy things taller than they are, stabbing in all directions. The only thing that's worse than two boys brandishing sticks is two boys brandishing sticks with a toddler wandering onto the lawn, which seems to happen every time someone comes round with more than one child, since the minute people have more than one they stop being obsessively protective and relax:

'Oh, don't worry about Thomas: he gets his eye poked out by his brother at home all the time.'

Oh, that's all right then.

In fact, the one reason I don't hate winter is because it's the season of No Sticks. They remain safely in the garden shed until the sun emerges blinking from hibernation and the first buds appear, heralding the start of spring – whereupon I don't think, *'Ah, the first buds! That'll be the start of spring.'* I think, *'Shit: any day now they'll be out in the garden with sticks.'*

And if you're wondering why I even *have* sticks, I have them because they're garden canes and I need them to tie to things. And besides, I'm not child-proofing the house at this stage, let alone the garden.

I didn't put those stupid clips on my cupboards, so I'm not letting my honeysuckle fall over because the Health and Safety police tell me to get rid of my sticks.

Instead, I prefer to periodically run out into the garden and try to stop Lawrence playing with them, convinced that someone, possibly my child, possibly *not* – which would obviously be *worse* – is going to get their eye poked out. And each time he looks amazed that I feel this way, as if on a loop of film that's gone back to the beginning. And each time, *I'm* amazed that he hasn't remembered everything I said last time.

Witness this exchange last summer, when his friend Michael came to play:

ME: [*on the phone*]: 'So there was this woman, saying to me, "My husband's crap in bed," and I'm like – "*Lawrence!* Give me that stick!"'

'Why?'

'Because you're going to poke Michael's eye out!'

'No, I'm not!'

Two minutes later, inside the back door:

'Michael? Are you all right?'

'Yes.'

'What's that mark near your eye?'

'Um. Lawrence – well, he—'

'LAWRENCE!!! GIMMETHATSTICKNOWRIGHT-NOWNOWNOW!!!'

'O-*K*!'

'Do you have any IDEA what will happen if Michael's mother comes to collect him, and I have to say, "He's had a lovely time, been very good: here's his eye IN A BAG"????'

Followed by the inevitable reply:

'But I didn't!'

Yeah, well. I've made my point. Or not.

Then, this year, something happens that challenges another of my so-called policies, in fact blows it right out of the water.

Anyone who knows me has heard me go on about how children must be allowed to develop their initiative and how as parents we need to reduce their dependency on us, and *our* dependency on their being dependent on us. And this being the most over-anxious generation of parents ever, this is particularly difficult. If I had said to my dad – who grew up with TB, diphtheria, polio, the Blitz, evacuation, no seat belts and no NHS, though not all in his family, just at the time generally – '*Can you collect me from a party on Saturday?*' I'd have got a clip round the ear. OK, no, I wouldn't, because he didn't go in for clipping. But I would have got his standard response to any kind of liberty taking:

'WHAT DO THINK THIS IS, A *HOTEL*??!!'

And so I'd leave the party early to get the bus, moaning. And I can say without fear of contradiction it's made me the nagging, bossy, control freak I am today.

But that's only the Outer Me. The Inner Me is a lovely person who nurtures her children with just the right blend of encouragement and detachment, so they can become increasingly autonomous and self-reliant, yet loving, trusting and able to express their needs. *In your dreams, matey.* Well, I did say Inner Me.

So here's the thing.

Peter, who claims to be one of the last generation to have asked each other, *'What did your dad do in the War?'* has had to come to terms with the fact that everyone does not share his obsession with that uniquely significant period in our nation's past, and that his children particularly don't.

Still, he has spent the past few months trying to get everyone he meets to read a book called *Taking Risks*, the memoir of Joseph Pell. Pell, born Epelbaum in Poland, was just fifteen when, on his way home one day in 1940, he saw German soldiers approaching the house. He crept away and hid in the barn, and then escaped to the forest where he met up with a band of partisans who lived on their wits, and centuries-old survival skills, until the end of the war. I mean, he actually had a gun and shot real Nazis. How Grown-up is that? It's a fantastic adventure story, truly inspiring, and those whom Peter does persuade to read it are gripped. He also tries to get the children interested, but to no avail.

That is, until Ray Mears covers the same topic. Going to tape David Attenborough, I notice I have a two-hour VHS and decide to bung on Mears's *Extreme Whittling* or whatever it is, as well. The kids have seen him before, and were pretty absorbed. Also, we need more videos. It's the epicentre of the Easter holidays, and worn out by running alongside the children while they rollerblade – their newest craze – we've been begging them to watch more TV.

I sit down with them and rewind. And there is Mears demonstrating the survival skills used by Jewish partisans in the war. It's as if the book has come to life.

He's not in Poland, but Belarus, where, just like Joseph Pell, hundreds of Jews ran away to join the partisans, in groups up to 1,200-strong, including women and children – basically anyone who got away, whether they were brave or not. Lawrence takes one look at an archive photo of a boy slightly older than himself with a rifle and is rapt. Lydia too.

'That is *so cool*.'

But it's not just the weapons that fascinate them. Mears makes a spoon out of a log – cue serious whittling – and they gasp with admiration.

'That is such a *cool spoon!*'

Then one of the Belarussian veterans he's come to meet makes Mears a pair of shoes out of lime bark. Then – wow! Mears shows how to get nutrition by finding an ants' nest and scooping the inhabitants and their grubs onto a tarpaulin or outspread coat.

'The ants rush to carry their larvae out of the sun,' he explains. 'Then all you have to do is collect them.' He makes a fire, using tinder and sticks. 'You can eat them raw, but fried with a little sugar they're even better – a bit like shrimp. Mmm!' The children love shrimp. They are staring, goggle-eyed, at the screen.

I think I might have found a way to keep them in one place, and also sublimate the desire for sticks.

'Hey, kids, why don't you play Partisans?'

Immediately, sofas are overturned, blankets draped. I whizz into the kitchen and poke about amongst the jars.

'Here are your forest berries.' I give them some raisins. 'And here are your ant grubs' (sunflower seeds). I add a bottle of water, congratulating myself on my imaginative resourcefulness.

'No thanks, Mummy,' says Lawrence. 'We're going

to collect our own from this pool.' He shows me a blue bowl he glazed at All Fired Up, which he's placed amongst the cushions. 'That's the pool, and these are the rocks.' He's wearing an orange throw from Ikea, tied diagonally across his chest. Lydia's in a vest, with a scarf worn as a sarong and another on her head. Plastic snakes and lizards, and the RSPB's fluffy owl and chaffinch – 'press here for authentic chirping' – are positioned around the room. They are completely absorbed and play this for the rest of the day.

When Peter comes in, I tell him proudly of my marvellous idea.

'And of course they're such great role models, these brave heroes and heroines. It really is fantastic, to see them playing like this. They're really thinking about what they'd do if they had to rely on their own resources.'

'Fantastic. Well done!'

Next door we can hear Lawrence quizzing Lydia as to her suitability for a more active role.

'Lydia, what's the one item you need the most for surviving in the forest?'

'A machete?'

'Good!'

The next day, Lawrence's friend Milo comes round and they give themselves code names and carry on the game in the garden. There are a few sticks involved, but they seem to be being broken up into less lethal lengths. They even allow Lydia to join in. Milo's mother Lucy and I retire peacefully to the kitchen, where I tell her about Joseph Pell, Ray Mears and the great partisan craze.

'They've just been riveted by it,' I say. 'It's so wonderful to see them out there, playing freely.'

'Absolutely,' says Lucy. 'Hang on – is your lawn on fire?'

We rush out and, sure enough, there's a pile of newspaper and sticks blazing merrily on the grass. She gets there before I do, and stamps it out.

'What's going on?!!'

'We did it with the magnifying glass.'

'You're kidding.'

'But—'

'But it's dangerous!'

Lawrence is totally crestfallen.

'You never want us to do *anything*.'

'No, I do. It's just . . .'

He slinks away in a sulk.

'You're very clever boys,' says Lucy. 'Really.'

'Yes, loads of initiative, which is brilliant. Just – er, be careful next time.'

I honestly am, I remind him at bedtime, very proud.

However, he's still a bit annoyed with me, and he's right. I want them to develop their initiative, but not *too much*.

'Look,' I tell him. 'If we ever do have to escape suddenly, bring your magnifying glass.'

Later that night Peter says, 'You know, if we ever did have to survive like that, the children might well be more resourceful than us.'

'Yeah?' I say. 'It's not like camping.'

Peter's vision of escaping and fighting the Nazis – as a kind of Jewish *Swallows and Amazons* – quite annoys me. Yet he's got me realizing that children's resourcefulness can be extraordinary. My father was exactly Lawrence's age when the war started. He was here, not in Europe, but was evacuated. The husband of the couple who took him tried to come in while he was having a bath, on the pretext of drying him. But Dad could tell, as one does, that it wasn't OK. So when he went to bed, he put a chair under the door handle. It's one reason why, on a bad day, I don't want Lawrence, or Lydia, ever to leave my sight. And it's why I'm glad he lit the fire.

9 Fear Is Not My Weapon

One thing that's always fascinated me is the great value adults attach to being brave, particularly in the young.

'Now, be brave!' they say to a child when they're about to do something unpleasant to him: pull off a plaster, shove in a hypodermic or tell him his puppy has died.

But why? In the case of the needle and the plaster, they surely want him to be *still*. As for death, the adult in that situation is presumably afraid of seeing the child cry. So shouldn't they tell *themselves* to be brave? And anyway, what's so terrible about crying? Quite apart from the known physiological benefit, it's a logical response to stress. And besides, if a child cries and you comfort him, you feel Effective. Having said that, I've remembered something I did once that shows just how easy it is to do the opposite of that, even when you don't mean to.

Many, many years after I left my primary school, but long before I had children, the mother of a friend of mine happened to take over as Head. She knew I'd been there, and invited me to come and have lunch with her, and look round. Since I hated it a great deal of the time, I was in two minds. To the Head in my day, infancy was an undesirable state. When she wanted to punish someone they were often threatened with being sent back to the nursery.

Yet nurseries are generally rather nice places, where you can paint and dress up and play with sand all day, and babyhood is heaven. You get fed on demand, all being well, you sleep when you like, and – my favourite part – you get wheeled around. I only wish I could remember it. It just wasn't so much fun being sent back there for half a day when you were seven. Anyhow, there I was being shown round by the new Head and thinking, as you do, how tiny the chairs looked, and how incredibly young the teachers. It was coming up to lunchtime, and just as in my day, there was no dining room; the teachers served the food to their classes in each open-plan class section. As we walked through the nursery bit there was a little boy, adorable in the red and grey uniform, his mini school jumper looking so cute. He was crying, so I knelt down and said, 'What's the matter?'

The teacher was unstacking the plates or something; she hadn't looked round. And the little boy said, 'I want my Mummy.'

And I said, 'She'll be here soon.'

But I realized as soon as I said it, I'd lied. That's to say, I knew even without being a parent yet that to a three-year-old, three hours can be like ten years. Also, I didn't know for a fact that it was his mother who'd be picking him up. But I said it automatically, as if programmed. Where did that come from? It was as if there was some pre-loaded, adult phrase book with an override mechanism that bypassed what I really felt. And yet the very reason I stopped in the first place was because I identified with him.

Achieving the right balance between strength and softness, like good lavatory paper, is surely one of the key things about caring for children. On the one hand, when they fall over it's good to acknowledge their pain and kiss it better. On the other hand, you don't want them hanging about endlessly with a slightly cut knee refusing to go to school and generally get on with their lives.

My parents were kind enough not to pooh-pooh those typical childhood fears, such as of the dark. We even had a special night light that always stayed on, on a sort of shelf above our bedroom door. Shadows, sinister outlines made by hung-up coats – anything like that – was, to use a favourite phrase of the government, a Legitimate Fear. They also managed, after they split up, to remember to collect us from school on the right days – sometimes quite a challenge for parents who've got a new and unfamiliar timetable in which they are alternately 'on' and 'off'. And we were never accidentally left alone for a whole weekend, like the younger son in *The Squid and the Whale*, to play with our mother's underwear and drink whisky. So *that's* good.

Just occasionally, though, we were alone for part of an evening at home. When that happened, my sister and I slept in Mum's bed. We liked the headboard, which was padded and covered with a striped material in different shades of blue. Also, instead of being in the centre of one wall with a gap on each side like other beds, the bed was snugly against the wall in one corner, where her bookshelf made a familiar landscape whose elements I checked off before going to sleep: Iona and Peter Opie's *Lore and Language of Schoolchildren*, orange and brown; Pablo Neruda, purple; Wallace Stevens, blue and white; W. Keble Martin's *Concise British Flora*, floral. Behind the wall was a concealed fireplace we weren't scared of, and whose existence we forgot about until years later, when a bird fell down the chimney and decomposed behind the headboard. Mum had a turquoise flannel dressing gown edged with white lace that we wrapped ourselves in before pulling up the covers, partly because it smelled nice, and partly to protect us from the wigstand.

Mum didn't wear wigs, but she did use hairpieces, fashion accessories to boost the 'built-up' look she preferred for going out. Back then, the late sixties and early seventies, almost everyone did their hair that way on dates or special occasions, with the hair curled, backcombed and pinned before being sprayed heavily, like a pile of thickly varnished dinner rolls. There were actually two wigstands, the good one and the evil one. The good one was shop-bought, with characterless features moulded in the same stuff they use to make dressmakers' dummies. It sat on the worktop and wished us no ill. The evil one had been sculpted by my mother out of polystyrene and painted with crudely gouged eye sockets circled with black and a mouth that gaped horribly. Like the other one it lived on the worktop, but unlike the other one it guarded the exit. During the day we walked past it many times, but came to no harm. At night, however, it assumed a malevolent power over us.

Because the bedroom was also her studio, the wall

opposite the bed had a narrow worktop running round it, as in a kitchen, with cupboards for huge sheets of paper underneath. To the left of the bed, the side you got in, was a peninsula of the same worktop, jutting out from the wall behind the bed all the way across the room, with a gap through which to walk in and out. The wigstand knew the gap was the only way out, but couldn't exert its powers beyond that area. So we were safe as long as we didn't need to go to the bathroom.

If the worst came to the worst, which it inevitably did, one of us had to run towards the wigstand and try to distract it while the other went for the door. It took a long time to work up the courage, with a lot of peering above the bedclothes, then losing our nerve. We planned our escapes minutely, going over every detail until we were sure we had a chance of survival. Coming back was nearly as bad.

I don't recall our ever disposing of it. It may have moved out when I did, or followed my mother to Kent. Maybe it's in a landfill site somewhere, buried but still sending its waves of evil through the soil. Polystyrene has a longer lifespan than plutonium,* so if your thing is to go digging on rubbish tips, don't say you haven't been warned.

* Or maybe not.

You may be reading this and thinking, *Bloody weirdo. That explains a lot.* And you'd probably be right. But let's not be too quick to dismiss children's fears. When my stepbrother Andrew was about three, he kept telling his parents he couldn't go to sleep because there was a 'beastie under the bed'. And they told him there wasn't, because they couldn't see it. Then one night they found his sister's pet mouse under there. So there.

I *wanted* to be able to say that with age, my fears have become more rational. I wanted so much to be fear-free that finding myself still frightened of anything is a bit of a blow – let alone things that most other people aren't scared of at all.

Years ago, my dad lived for a while down a somewhat isolated lane in Kent, and almost as soon as we got in the car at this end, I'd be trying to think what to do if I saw a spider. In the old, dusty house the silence magnified every creak. I dreaded bedtimes, and would put off going to the loo for ages, edging into the bathroom *very* slowly like the NYPD, in case there was one lying in wait. As the sink was their other favourite venue, I also lived in fear of the washing-up, though, as you can imagine, this was thought to be just an excuse. I'd feel sick if I saw a big one, and to his credit Dad was quite sympathetic. He understood the terror they pro-

voked in us, and tried to alleviate it with a mural called
'Silly Spiders' which he drew on our bedroom wall, in
which one spider was asking another, *'How many little
girls have you frightened today?'* When the fear of creepy-
crawlies *and* the dark reached saturation levels, I pulled
up the covers and tried to sleep completely sealed in,
poking out my nose every few minutes to breathe.

My mother lives in a village quite near Dad's old
place, though hers isn't at all, to use one of Claire's
words, *webby*. One weekend we are visiting, and it's all
going well. She and I aren't shouting at each other,
which is nice. And the children are playing happily. She
and they get on very well – it's only a matter of skipping
a generation – and we've reached the point where Peter
and I can nip out to the pub without something happening that she can't handle.

Currently they are carefully emptying her jars of
lentils, chickpeas, etc. into bowls, and weighing them.
I am upstairs, staring at myself in the mirror. Can I go
to the pub with this little make-up on? Should I add
another layer? The lights are quite bright in there.
Hmm. Suddenly there's a flurry of activity at the bottom of the stairs.

'What?!'

'Um, you'd better not look, Mummy.'

'Why? What is it?'

Peter is in firefighter mode, shepherding people around the ground floor of the house.

'Right! Get me a glass.'

'What is it??'

Lawrence tries to break it to me gently.

'Um, Mummy. It's a spider, OK?'

Lydia charges breathlessly up the stairs.

'A HUGE spider! It's MASSIVE.'

'And – well, I'm just saying, Mummy: DON'T LOOK.'

I clutch the side of the basin. My knees feel weak.

The definition of courage, I read somewhere, is not not being afraid; it's not showing fear in front of others.

'Is it – *big*?'

'Put it this way, Mummy: VERY.'

'OK. Just don't show it to me, OK?'

But I have failed to grasp that it is already *up here*. The flurry of excitement downstairs is due to having to find a glass. Like *Alien*, it is Already On the Ship.

Peter doesn't kill them – I wouldn't ask him to. So he has to have his spider-wrangling kit of a Glass & Postcard. I think, in a phobics' village as designed by Prince Charles, it might be the pub. He has to get the glass over the spider, then slide the postcard . . . uh-oh!

'Please don't bring it near me! Please! Please! Oh, *please*!'

I am desperate. I am shaking. But out of the corner of my eye, I peer – *why*, I don't know – at the *thing* in the glass. It is BIG. It has eight legs. And it is coming towards me.

'OMIGOD. Getitawaygetitawaygetitaway!!!!!!!! *Arrgh*!'

They rush it past me, like doctors in *ER*. But even then I see it under the glass and feel wobbly and sick. Peter sighs heavily.

'I thought we agreed,' he says as he comes back upstairs, 'that you wouldn't show the children your fear. So they wouldn't become infected by it.'

'Well, *sorry*. I can "not show my fear" if it's normal-sized. Not if it's bigger than I am.'

He says children 'catch' arachnophobia from their parents, but that's just not true. My mother will sit down and chat to a spider – or bat, or bug – before drawing it. She had a frozen bat in her freezer for years. My father wasn't quite so keen on the eight-legged visitors, but no way ever jumped onto a chair screaming. And Lawrence and Lydia have communed with tarantulas, met them socially and held them in the palms of their hands. The only reason I've been able to not show my fear so far is because we live in a largely spider-free zone. When they met the tarantulas, at the amazing Tropiquaria in Somerset, I went outside for an ice cream. I was cornered by a pretty big one at home once – not tarantula, house spider – when I came in late one night, but no one else saw it and Peter was asleep so I had to leave it there. I crept back up the stairs without my late-night drink – it was blocking the way to the wine rack, and spent the next month or so surreptitiously peering round the door every time I came in.

And can I just say, by the way, that while I confess to having put fifty yards between myself and the Mexican red-kneed tarantula, called, if I remember rightly, Tina, I did cuddle one of their boa constrictors. Surely that should count for something. Should I put it on my CV, perhaps, or drop it into any situations that involve conflict or negotiations: *'Well, as I've found when handling the South American boa constrictor ...'*

And surely it should make up a *little* bit for the fact that I don't like thunder or the dark, though at least with the latter I can cover my fear by giving way to the children's nightly plea to have the landing light on. Thunder is a bit trickier. Whenever they've come running into our room because of it, and so can personally witness my pathetic reaction, I try very hard to convince them that when I leap into the air whimpering, I'm doing it as a joke.

Well, OK, maybe Peter's right and parents are sometimes *a bit* to blame. I realize this after the debacle with *Jurassic Park 2*. The stupid thing is, I'm not even supposed to be watching it. He and Lawrence and Lydia are. Then I happen to wander in and notice one of my favourite actors, Richard Schiff, who plays Toby Ziegler in *The West Wing*. So I abandon whatever activity I'm meant to be involved in – attaching name tapes or reading an improving book – and sit down. But things aren't going well for Toby. Having got his state-of-the-art T-rex-busting weapon lined up, and demonstrated its efficiency, he becomes trapped in his jeep, the gun jams, and he is torn apart by *two* T-rexes who take one half each. I become so distressed by the sight of President Barlet's chief speech writer being turned into a human wishbone that I run from the room wailing, whereupon Lydia, who's been watching calmly, bursts into tears.

'Well done,' said Peter, as if I've deliberately set out to ruin her enjoyment of the film.

I *could* have said, 'Did it occur to you that she might not be *ready* for people being torn limb from limb in their own jeeps? Even those who haven't gained international recognition as the sincere stalwarts of highly respected political dramas?' But being the tactful, supportive spouse that I am, I merely confine myself to pulling his footstool away.

Some months after this, he asks: 'Are they ready to see *Terminator*, do you think?'

'Well, considering that Lydia's current reading matter involves plucky little ponies rescuing people from lakes, and her DVD choice tonight is *The Magic Roundabout* and not homicidal androids who, after being blown to smithereens in hails of bullets, reconstitute themselves from pools of liquid metal, probably not.'

'I only asked. What about Lawrence, then?'

Lawrence is another kettle of eels. When he and I went to see *King Kong*, which I'd kept Lydia well away from, he was like a rock. All through the sequences with the terrifying, malevolent islanders, sequences which had me and other adults waking afterwards, sweating in the night, he didn't flinch. When they started decapitating the crew I put my hands over his face but he fought me off. As other, older children were carried out trembling, he watched impassively, appreciating the editing. Then, during the orgiastic massacre in the ravine, as I shook all over, he let me hold his hand.

'It's all right, Mummy,' he soothed. 'I'm used to this sort of thing.'

Well, if grizzled sailors having their heads bitten off by huge, phallic worms has recently been added to the National Curriculum, then hooray. At this rate he won't just be able to watch *Terminator*. He can earn extra pocket money as my minder. I scare easily, and it clearly isn't getting any better.

What's even more unimpressive, though, is that I occasionally *forget*. I revert to my fantasy self who loves lone travel, mountaineering and paragliding, and is any day now going to get a very small boat and a faulty navigation system and sail single-handedly round the world. Away from home, I become particularly susceptible to forgetting what a feeble specimen I really am. Just as I imagine that because I look as though I come from there, I might magically be able to speak Greek or Italian, I get deluded by the sheer foreignness of my surroundings into believing I'm brave. Peter and I had a fantastic holiday in Montserrat years ago, before it was buried under lava obviously, and everything about it was perfect except for the day a very charming girl we met offered to get her friend to take us up in his plane. Instead of saying, '*Small plane, seats four? No, thank you!*' I got in, and then was exceedingly disappointed to hear a voice – mine – whimpering: 'Oh no! Oh no!' for more or less the entire half an hour. With every little dip and buffet, I was convinced we were going to fall out of the sky, and the heartfelt 'Thank You!!' with which I said goodbye to the pilot was mainly due to relief that we had come down. But at least that was before I had kids.

On holiday in Madeira two years ago, when the kids were five and six, Lydia and I went off together one day after lunch, leaving Peter and Lawrence behind. At the front of the town was a cable-car terminus which she excitedly identified and before I knew it, I found myself standing in the queue. *Hang on*, I said to myself, *you're AFRAID OF HEIGHTS. That's OK*, said my other voice, *it's obviously quite a small one that doesn't go very far.*

All the same, I did try to interest her in coming back another day, preferably with Daddy. But she would have none of it. We got on, and as we did so, I could see for the first time just how far the thing went: right up the mountain behind the capital, over a motorway and into the hinterland beyond. For all I knew, it went all the way to Spain.

'Um, Lydia, I'm not sure I can do this. I – you see, I'm not very good with heights.'

'Oh, please, Mummy! PLEASECANWEPLEASE-CANWEPLEASEPLEASEPLEASEPLEASEPLEASE????'

The frozen expression of terror on my face as it moved away is captured for posterity in the photograph they take and present to you when you make it back down again – if you haven't had a stroke. Needless to say, the whole thing was made doubly humiliating by Lydia saying periodically, 'It'll be all right, Mummy, don't worry,' as I gripped the edge of my seat, willing it not to sway, while the German couple who shared it with us took it in turns to glance away from viewing the great void below to laugh at my amusing weakness in the face of something so obviously unfrightening as being suspended in a moving glass box hundreds of feet above the ground. At least we wouldn't have to come back the same way, as the nice Madeirans plied their traditional trade of pulling tourists along the streets in wicker sledges from exactly the point where the cable car stopped. It being February, however, the season hadn't begun.

I thought, I really did, that I would grow out of that. Grown-ups are supposed to define themselves by their peer group, so a fear is rational if everyone else is frightened of it, and irrational if you're the only one. The kids' schools send home hectoring letters about sunblock because everyone is frightened of skin cancer, but if you read up on the causes of malignant melanomas, you discover that UV light at the strength you get it in the UK isn't one of them. Cars kill sixty times more children a year than strangers, but which are parents more scared of?

Adults may not have to be fear*less*, but are nonetheless meant to be afraid of the right things, the things we all agree are 'scary'.

Appropriately, as I am pondering this, the DVD of *Batman Begins* plops onto the mat, tagline: *Fear is Your Weapon*. Lawrence and I have been eagerly anticipating this, one of several that Peter has decreed Too Scary For Lydia, and by an unusual piece of luck, Peter is with his mate in Brighton – we haven't had a row this time, he's just having a night away – and Lydia is staying the night with a friend. It's starring Christian Bale, whom I loved in *Empire of the Sun*. We settle down comfortably, with our drinks and crisps.

The whole of the first part consists of Bruce Wayne being beaten up by way of initiation by some ninja types in a mountain fortress, presided over by Liam Neeson. It's a bit like that flashback in *Die Another Day* when James Bond is tortured by the North Koreans, except without the tension, brevity or pace. This actually *is* like being tortured by the North Koreans. Despite a robe-like garment and a drooping moustache, Liam Neeson looks bizarrely out of place, like a fundraiser for the Republicans in a dressing gown. Did you ever see the TV series with David Carradine, *Kung Fu*? It spawned a million spoofs and is the one where his teacher called him Grasshopper. This is sillier. Flash back to Wayne's childhood. He falls into a well, and is menaced by bats. I go out for more wine and, while I'm at it, another two bags of crisps. When I come back, he's still down there. Lawrence is watching intently. Bruce's father, Wayne Senior, who's supposed to be some kind of genius, eventually gets him out and says:

'Bruce, why do we fall? [*Undramatic pause*] So we can get up!'

'Dear God . . .' I say.

Lawrence says, 'Sssh!'

The man is then shot by one of those grizzled, twitching muggers who only appear in *Batman* and *Spiderman* films. He hands over his wallet willingly but is killed anyway, along with Bruce's mother, to show us that the streets of Gotham are paved with Evil, and this is, after all, based on a comic.

Back, or rather forward, to Liam, in the robe, up the mountain, with the drooping moustache. Bruce takes a good deal of trouble to get to the top to collect a unique blue flower, which Liam then crushes in a bowl.

'Breathe in your Fear,' he tells Bruce, stabbing at it with his ninja's pestle. 'To conquer Fear,' he continues momentously, 'you must *become* Fear.'

He then brings forward a murderer who must be executed. Bruce must show he has breathed in and conquered fear by stabbing him through the neck with a fire poker. But, being a goody, and soon – though not *nearly* soon enough – to be Batman, he refuses.

'If you kill, you become like them,' he says, looking, I notice now, very like Christopher Reeve.

'The city has become a breeding ground for suffering and injustice,' says Liam, moustache twitching. I go out for more wine, and find it a good moment to clean some of the kitchen cupboards. When I come back he seems to be intoning, 'Al Gore rescued us from the darkness of our hearts.'

'*Al Gore?!*'

'Ssssh!' says Lawrence.

'That can't be right, surely.'

'Just shut up, will you?'

Lawrence faithfully watches the whole thing, right through the interminable building of the Batsuit, Batmobile and other Batgear, through Michael Caine ageing from quite old, loyal retainer Alfred to very old loyal retainer, and Morgan Freeman wasting his career in the basement of Wayne Tower.

Eventually it ends. And I have this to say. If only Fear were as boring as this. Then I too could breathe it in and conquer it.

10 Very Long Multiplication

In *Confessions of a Bad Mother* I told Lawrence: 'I want another job than picking things up all the time!' to which he replied: 'You have another job: giving out drinks.'

Despite my ongoing attempt to show that (a) I do not derive all my personal fulfilment from being their waiter and (b) I actually have a life outside in which I deploy other skills, my children are convinced that I exist to serve them. And these are not particularly spoiled kids. They are kind and empathetic and clever and frequently utterly sweet. But they do think I was put on earth to attend to their every whim. And how will they ever therefore become self-sufficient?

One of the promises I've made to myself for my impending old age is to have brought up two children who will actually be able to perform basic tasks for themselves, and not be like the young Jessica Mitford who left home not knowing you had to pay for electricity. Mind you, she did then run away to the Spanish Civil War, where it was a bit less of an issue. As I've explained to Lydia, the problem with Very Good Mothers is they tend to do everything for their children, and then their children never learn to do anything for themselves. They get so spoiled and selfish that they go from one flatshare to another, getting booted out of all of them for never cleaning the shower and using up all the milk. Or they don't learn to function independently at all, and end up living at home until their parents die, and even beyond that, in cardigans. And she has duly taken this point on board, although not to the extent that she ever picks up her clothes. Witness, in this exchange between a mother and toddler at the swimming baths, how it all begins:

CHILD: 'You dropped my sock.'

MOTHER: 'Yes, sorry. Aren't I a silly billy? Isn't Mummy a silly billy?'

CHILD: 'Yes you are!'

ME: Hey, kid! Pick up your own damn sock.

OK, I didn't say it out loud. But what is it about motherhood in particular that has to manifest itself with such servility? Where in the dictionary does it say '*mother = servant*'? And in the face of such devoted service, how are our offspring ever to grow up them-selves?

I'd also like to have reached the point sometime in the next twenty years, and before I'm too old to even *move*, where I get some Time Off. Perceptively, you will have noticed that these two things are related. So: I am trying to get them to *help*.

I'm doing them a favour. One day they'll have to fend for themselves, so they need to know how to pick up a pair of socks.

You see? I am starting with something Manageable.

'Lawrence, I really need you to put your dirty clothes in the wash.'

'OK. But I've got a lot on my mind!'

'Like what?'

'The eight times table, what school I go to . . .'

'Be that as it may. You agreed to put your clothes in the wash if I gave you a rise in pocket money, and you haven't.'

'But I'm so tired . . .'

'Well, how d'you think I feel?'

'You get to laze around all day.'

'Well, actually . . .'

'And anyway, I'm not your *slave*.'

Where did he get that phrase, I wonder?

'You were supposed to do it last night. That's the deal.'

'I'm not your SLAVE!!!'

Certainly, if God came down tomorrow and said, *'I can remove one irritation from your life which you don't want and make it disappear forever; what'll it be?'* I would choose Picking Stuff Up Off the Floor, because it is this that most frequently sends me off the scale. It's not just that my back has RSI from the bending; it's that two seconds after I've said, *'Please pick your things up,'* both children will come past, and – as if delivering a visual punchline à la Laurel & Hardy – drop something on the floor. It's then not only On the Floor, but On the Floor in the Wrong Room. By teatime they'll have managed to redistribute 75 per cent of their belongings round the house, like badly applied socialism.

There are drawings in the bathroom, swimming towels on the stairs, school reading books behind the beds and – my pet hate – cheese string wrappers like a new micro-accessory all over the sofa. And let's not forget Lydia's soft toys. The members of this portable menagerie migrate – not seasonally, but without warning. Puppy feeling insecure in Lydia's room? He comes for a weekend break in ours – and forgets to go back. Unicorn doesn't like the ambience in the bedroom? She sets up home in the kitchen. It's like Gerald Durrell with stuffing. The only thing you can say in their favour is that unlike real animals, if you grab them by the tail and hurl them up the stairs, they don't mess up the carpet.

This reaches a certain point, generally about an hour after we've got home, where I get a teensy bit *fed up*.

'Pick your things up! Pick your things up! Pick your THINGS UP!!!'

And they'll look up in wonderment, like anthropologists hearing an entirely new language.

'There's no need to get SHIRTY.'

'WELL, *DO IT THEN!!!!!*'

And this isn't even counting the things under the kitchen table: squashed broccoli florets, for example, cold pasta and *glitter*.

And the sitting room is constantly being dismantled. I often stagger in there with a nice big box that contained a computer part or another recently released item from Peter's past, to come back later and find them playing happily beside it – amongst the various parts of the sofa. It didn't matter when it was a posh room that no one ever went in, but since we started actually using it, it's a nuisance. You come in with a glass in your hand, rushing not to miss the start of

Shameless, and find you have to reassemble the furniture. It's *Groundhog Day* in Ikea. I've got nothing against dens – am all in favour, in fact – but I'd quite like once just to be able to come in and sit down.

Never mind that I'm also trying to thread the loose beads back onto Lydia's bracelet and tie the ends of that infuriating slippery plastic string together, put her toast on at exactly two on the dial so it's not too crispy – she checks – speed up with the drinks, and watch Lawrence play a game on the computer so mind-bendingly repetitive that after five minutes of it you want to rip your own head off; I'm sure if you made Al Qaeda watch it a few times they'd tell you their schedule for the next twenty years. And all this is just part of a 'quick play' before homework.

And it is in this mode that I attempt to help Lawrence with his maths.

I am actually quite looking forward to this, because I was once Good at Maths. I enjoyed it at primary school, and when I started at secondary did well in my first test, so was put in the A stream. Four years later, I failed my mock O level. Amazing what teaching can do. Anyway. I am relishing the prospect of getting back into some numbers.

'We have to do all these,' says Lawrence with a despondent wave of the hand.

'What, the whole sheet?'

'YES!!'

'Right. Long multiplication. Let's see ... OK, you times that by that, then that by that ...'

It goes reasonably well. He can do them OK, as long as he takes it one step at a time and doesn't panic or rush, which is a bit of a challenge, since *The Simpsons* is only forty minutes away. And anyway, the homework's supposed to take twenty, which is frankly absurd. Still we carry on. The only thing is, some of the numbers are very, very large.

'That six doesn't seem to be quite lined up with the others. Why's that?'

'I don't know! I've only got eighteen minutes left!'

'And that seventeen there ...'

'How should I know?!'

We get three-quarters of the way through, then realize we've been incorporating the question numbers into the sums.

'Why on earth have they put them so close together?' I say. 'That's ridiculous!'

'You can't say that, Mummy! They're the School.'

He puts his head on the table, and I send him off to watch *The Simpsons*, because it really isn't his fault.

'We're going to have to do that whole lot again,' I moan to Peter, who says, 'It'll be fine.'

Stronger men than I have ended up in tears over homework. Part of me doesn't care and just wants it to Go Away. No, it's not that, it's if I ever *do* want them to grow up and be independent, they'll have to start learning not to be bailed out. No, I don't want them to get low marks, but they are *their* marks ultimately, not mine. When Lawrence left his homebook behind the other day, and I knew I was going past the school, I dithered for a while then didn't bring it. I had a vision of myself turning up in the future at his office with his laptop or Blackberry, and then taking notes for him, then gradually taking over completely. Then I'd be one of those mothers I promised myself I would never be, like the woman I read about in the paper who drove to Scotland to give her son his PlayStation. And I would have to shoot myself.

So clearly homework has a use. My father often pointed that out. When I moaned about it, and he told me that Grown-ups also had to do stuff they don't like, I didn't believe him.

'I have to do stuff I don't like all the time,' he'd say.

'No, you don't. Like what?'

'Paying tax. Getting the car serviced. Paying bills. Working hard to earn money then having to spend it on boring things like divorce.' This being not a reference to my mother but to No. 2.

'Yeah, but you don't have to spend a Sunday evening doing French lit.'

In the list of things I don't miss from seven years of secondary education, Racine's rhyming couplets come pretty near the top. But at least I know how to work on my own. I can sit at my desk eating biscuits and swapping mpegs just as well as anyone in an office.

Coincidentally, like me, Lydia doesn't find it easy to finish things. She daydreams. A lot. So tasks don't get completed.

'Lydia, can you finish your story, please?'

'In a minute.'

Half an hour later:

'Lydia, can you finish your story?'

'I'm doing it!'

Ten minutes later:

'Lydia! Finish your BLOODY STORY!'

'ALL RIGHT! CAN'T YOU STOP NAGGING ME FOR ONCE?!!!'

If she was God, by Day 7 she'd still be on the lighting. It'd be really wonderful lighting, but – you know. A bit lacking in species.

I know I can't be doing her stories for her, or Lawrence's sums. So I end up shouting at her to Get

On With It because I can't bear her distress when she doesn't. Yet I know that in the end I have to leave her to it. I can't follow her into exams, or to university and sit behind her through her tutorials, or accompany her to work and tell her what to say in meetings. Did Mozart's mother play the piano for him? Did Galileo's stand beside the telescope with a tray of olives, dropping hints? Did – oh, you know what I mean.

'I can't do *anything*,' she says eventually, flinging herself across the table. 'Just Slow Writing.'

'Yes, you can!' I say. 'You can draw, do maths, spell. You're a brilliant speller. Anyhow, I never wrote enough at school either. Never came top in English or any of that. And look at me now.'

She puts her head on one side and peers at me impatiently.

'What about you?'

'I'm a writer. So it doesn't matter. You're OK!'

She rolls her eyes theatrically in the way she does when I'm being particularly dense.

'No, you're not, Mummy.'

'Really? What am I, then?'

'You're a *typer*. You type. Writing's done with a *pencil*.'

*

I must make a note to give up trying to set myself up as any kind of example. It's too hard on the ego, for a start. It's also beginning to dawn on me that one of the lessons of growing up, as a parent, is actually accepting, not just knowing, that you really can't fix everything for them. You have to embrace autonomy, by degrees, and *let go*. I should know this. I *do* know this. I fought for independence pretty hard myself.

Is this Growing Up? I don't know, but it's a terrifying thought; so much so that I decide to put it out of my head completely and go back to nagging.

11 The Cushion of Doom

Outside the office of Lawrence's headmaster, there's this cushion. It's where the boys have to sit if they've done something really naughty, and I have this feeling that no matter how hard I try, sooner or later I'm going to end up on it. The other day I was a bit early for Lawrence, so I sneaked in to use the loo. This dinner lady saw me, and I was absolutely sure she was going to tell me off.

'I'm just going to the loo,' I said. And she said, 'It's just there,' even though I knew this as I was standing right outside it.

A couple of weeks ago, the Head found me in the corridor trying to work out, like Alice in Wonderland, which of the many doors led to the information I wanted about next term's school trip. He said, 'Can I help?' and I nearly put up my hands. I said, 'I'm looking for – Mrs – er . . .'

He smiled. Was he being nice, or smiling in anticipation of the fatal blunder that would lead me to the Cushion?

'The Head of Year 5!'

Phew. He insisted on taking me there, and I had to come up with enough sane conversation to last about thirty-eight seconds. I blame all those World War Two films. When I get into that place I become gripped by a weird sort of desire for subterfuge mixed with panic – as if I'm going to have to dive into a store cupboard and come out disguised as the Head of Geography.

Even when I'm supposed to be there it happens. On Parents' Evening, for example. Peter and I file in with the Proper Parents, the bankers and lawyers and people who know what a hedge fund is, the backbone of society, and I can tell he's also thinking: *Any minute now they're going to pull us out of the line.* One of those doors probably leads to a rubbish chute. The steely-eyed rugby teacher will give a nod to the caretaker, and in six months we'll turn up in prison sausages. I look up at the board, where the names of boys who've won various cups are painted on in gold. It goes all the way back to 1911. 'Look up there!' I hiss at Peter. 'The last name is missing. What have they done to him?!' Peter glances upwards.

'It's 2007. It hasn't been put up yet.'

'Oh.'

We linger at a discreet distance from Lawrence's teacher's table, near enough to let her know we're waiting, but not so near we're in danger of hearing her explaining to the couple in front of her that their son is a genius/psychopath/not likely to be running the World Bank in two years after all. When it's our turn I smile broadly, but within reason, obviously – not like a nun on Ecstasy – on the grounds that it will at least start us off on the right foot. There's no reason to be nervous, I tell myself. These people only have youth, energy, experience and further education on their side. And, even if they don't like our child, maybe they'll feel a smidgeon of sympathy for us.

And it was incredibly neurotic of me to worry because, as Peter never tires of pointing out, it's All Fine.

Which is just as well, because the people who really make me anxious at school are the other mothers. Coming into the playground, I overhear a group of them *arranging something*.

'OK, I'll collect you and we'll go together.'

'What time?'

'Seven thirty. But Annie can't get there till eight.'

And so on.

Fair enough. Why not? But all I can think is, '*Why haven't they invited me?*' even when they're people who live near each other and not near me so it's all Totally Fine and Normal. I still feel I have to sort of skirt round them so they won't think I want to join in, because that's worse, isn't it? Far worse than not being invited is looking as if you want to be. There's a sort of dodge I can do, behind the equipment shed, and if I'm spotted by anyone, I can laugh and pretend it's a joke.

Rationally I know it isn't important, that I'm truly not that insecure. And I'm sure if I overheard them in a supermarket, or anywhere else, it wouldn't be so bad. But because it's the playground, I immediately whizz back to the third year, when I was at my most uncool. The playground is a kind of crucible that blends awful childhood memories and female hormones, I suppose, with potentially explosive effects.

The third year of school was not my best. I went to an incredibly cool school, but at fourteen, when the others were wearing Biba tops and the right brand of jeans – Levis, Inega, or even Fioruccis, which were obscenely expensive at £21 if you follow these things – I had *Brutus*. They say if you watch *Grange Hill* everyone looked hideous in the seventies, but there were *levels*. At least it wasn't a bitchy school; our class used to hug and kiss each other goodbye every Friday, and when it came to the holidays some of us cried. But I still wanted to be slim and clever, and to have as much money as them. I really, really wanted to Get It Right, and I never did. Now I don't give a shit about who's got a better car or jeans or handbag, but I still want them to like me.

Whenever I'm stuck in my Third Year time warp, I moan to Peter. After about twelve minutes of it, his sympathy dries up.

'Mmm, well my school was ruled by a boy called Wilson who one day made sixteen other boys line up against a wall because he *felt like it.*'

He went to school in 1960s Sheffield, incidentally, not 1930s Berlin.

'Yeah, well that's no use to me.'

'I'm just saying it could be worse.'

'Well, thanks for listening.'

'You do actually have friends.'

'Yeah. Miles away.'

'Not this again . . .'

'And another thing: did you know Amy and Tom are going on holiday with the Andrews?'

'So?'

'The Andrews! They never ask *us.*'

'Well, thank God. He only ever talks about the single currency and she's obsessed with schools. You don't *want* to go on holiday with them. We went there for dinner and you ended up locked in the lavatory in tears.'

'That wasn't because of them, it was those other people. Anyway I'd just like to be asked. I mean, what's wrong with us?'

I hear the unmistakeable rustle of a newspaper being opened.

'Fine. OK.' I take out the corkscrew and bang the drawer shut, whereupon it opens again. Even the furniture is against me.

12 Art For Fuck's Sake

You remember all those hideous child-development charts that tell you what they *should* be doing at five months, one year and so on? Would they be seen for the harbingers of despondency that they are if they were also published for adults?

Age 18: Able to order a round. Votes Labour. Prefers extremely loud music. Wears trousers that don't come up to anywhere near the waist. At first sign of sun rushes outside to remove clothes. Mistrustful of police, in favour of underdressed teenage girls. Able to have sex without extensive mental or cosmetic preparation, or removing clothes.

25: Should be reading a broadsheet newspaper, probably the *Guardian* or *Independent*, not living with parents, in full-time work. Able to drive. If man, in favour of underdressed teenage girls but able to go out with same female for more than a year.

30: Should be able to eat one or two chocolates without devouring whole box. In a job with prospects and serious relationship, perhaps considering marriage. Own car. Gets first mortgage. Begins to consider night-clubs too noisy. Starts to watch some BBC4.

40: Should be a parent, in stable relationship, in own home. Starts to be irritated by local pubs causing a nuisance at night. Slows down when passing garden centres. At first sign of sun rushes outside to hang up bird feeders. Beginning to prefer alcohol to drugs. Tells partner to hurry up and finish before *Desperate House-wives* comes on.

50: Starts to read *Daily Telegraph* at weekends. Shakes head disapprovingly at other drivers. At first sign of sun rushes out to mow lawn. Picks up other people's litter while tutting. Sends correctly punctuated text mes-sages. Gets first reading glasses. Reassured by presence of police, pretends to be appalled by underdressed teenage girls. First divorce.

*

60: Reads *The Times* or the *Daily Telegraph* regularly. Goes to the opera. Experiences soreness in knees while going up stairs. Chooses shoes for comfort, dismisses contemporary music as tuneless. Rejects sex with spouse in order to finish favourite book. Begins to watch simpler television, e.g. *Midsomer Murders* or A *Touch of Frost.* Joins the National Trust.

70: Reads the *Sunday Telegraph*, votes Conservative. Wears trousers that come up to well above the waist. Visits gardens on National Open Gardens Day. May go on a cruise. Books sex with spouse or partner if still awake at the end of *Gardeners' World*. Starts to read ads at the back of *Sunday Express* magazine.

80: Reads the *Sunday Express* all the way through. Buys first trousers with elasticated waistbands from ad in the back. Finds television adaptations of Agatha Christie intellectually stimulating. Says, 'Thank you, driver!' when getting off a bus.

Remembering the demoralizing effect these charts had on me, I reflect how handy it is that *not* forcing kids onto the next stage all the time chimes perfectly with my Do Less Philosophy. After all, children who aren't endlessly pushed do actually Grow Up. They don't just lapse into a corner with their mouths hanging open until they go into a retirement home. Pushing is all very well for overly high-powered parents who see everything in terms of productivity and just can't relax, but they remind me of drivers who rev their engines at red lights. You just want to get out and say to them, *'Get your foot off and stop wasting petrol, you twat!'* Do they go home to their gardens and stand over the flowers, hassling them to open? Personally, I Can't Be Arsed. But I call it my Do Less Philosophy since it sounds more Blairish and *proactive*, and less, well, Can't Be Arsed.

Peter and I frequently get up in the mornings and congratulate ourselves on our laid-backness. From not getting them to feed themselves to not teaching them to read, we've never dragged the children onto whichever stage they're 'supposed' to be at. We've also never felt they should be doing all those extra activities – piano, violin, ballet, rugby, chess, corporate finance – that the middle classes are now obsessed with, which drain the bank balance while making the child feel constantly obliged to perform. Never mind the dent it makes in your social life. 'I can't come out to dinner,

I have to pick William up from cricket' is a sentence I intend never to utter – not least because neither of my children is named William. We have even remained completely unbothered about the lack of Proper Culture in their lives. That is until the mother of one of Lydia's classmates – in Reception, this is – tells me she and her son go every Sunday to the Tate Modern.

'It's great for kids. Luke loves it!'

And he's a whole year younger than Lawrence. And she is not, by the way, some pushy, my-son-is-going-to-be-the-next-Charles-Saatchi nightmare person. She is, in fact, more laid back than I am. The shame! The embarrassment! I went to galleries as a child. Well, a bit. Now my children sit around all weekend eating Cheestrings and doing colouring in on the Captain Underpants website. In their pants. Conclusion: our children are babyish philistines. How have I let this happen? Seeing as I grew up with two parents who drew for a living, and a stepmother who did etchings on the kitchen table, often literally, the lack of Art in my children's lives really *is* a disgrace. They do some at school, of course. And they have piles of paper and pens to draw whenever the urge takes them at home. But we never go to galleries. And I feel if there's one aspect of their upbringing my father would probably be bothered about, Up There in artists' heaven with all the Playboy bunny angels and free pencils, it's that. Suddenly the Do Less Philosophy is in the bin.

I tell Peter: 'We never see any Art! Why don't we?'

He says, 'We went to the Design Museum to hear that talk.'

This was by Ken Adam, who designed *The Ipcress File, Dr Strangelove* and most of the James Bond films. The children weren't there.

'That doesn't count.'

'Has someone at school been winding you up again?'

'Don't be silly! I was just talking to Jan, and—'

'Oh, for God's sake.'

'No! Honestly! We must do this. I went to galleries as a child. It's a whole side of life they're missing. A whole dimension. We really must make the effort.'

From behind the bathroom door I can hear the softly turning pages of a car magazine. This is the man, you should know, who on holiday in San Sepolcro steered me away from the Piero della Francesca museum and into an ironmonger's.

'Mmm.'

'Peter? Don't you think?'

'Absolutely.'

'Good! That's settled then.'

'Does it involve leaving the house on a Sunday?'

I ring Claire, who says: 'I hardly go either. I'll meet you at the National Gallery and we can take Lawrence to that show for children.'

This is 'Tell Me a Picture', a show of pictures chosen by Quentin Blake, with notes and signposts by him, designed to entice kids into the perfectly accessible world of 'grown-up' Art. Lawrence is five at this point, and I reckon more than ready. He certainly draws a lot, mainly multi-limbed aliens with integral, high-resolution weaponry.

We meet at 'Tell Me a Picture', and start going round.

'Look, Lawrence, that's a painting by . . .'

He gets through the alphabet surprisingly quickly. In fact, he's passed T before we've even finished looking at C. He gets to the end and announces, 'I'm hungry. You said we could have a cake.'

Though a lover of cake as much as the next woman, Claire looks a little taken aback. We've been round the entire show in less than four minutes.

'Well, it's a start,' she says brightly.

I decide to abandon the whole project for another year.

Then we get a leaflet from our local gallery about classes for children.

'Hey, children! Art classes! What do you think?'

Lawrence looks round warily and says, 'Saturday's my Day Off.'

Lydia's quite keen, but she's below the minimum age. So we go to Tate Modern, and they both love it.

'Mum! Dad! This is GREAT!!'

Half an hour after our arrival they show no sign of wanting to leave the huge long slope down to the entrance, which they are charging up and down at great speed, not at all bored.

'It's even better than the Science Museum!'

The Science Museum has a pretty good slope, which turns a sharp corner and is so popular we have to ration the number of goes on it to ten or we never see anything else. It is at least, though, inside the building. Tate Modern's is outside, meaning that it's quite possible we will never actually make it as far as the Art.

'Kids! Shall we go inside?'

'We don't want to!!'

Finally we take their hands and, to the slightly perturbed glances of tourists, pull them firmly inside.

The permanent collection doesn't grab me at all.

'Look, kids! Isn't this great?'

Luckily there's a temporary show on featuring a pile of rubbish – tin cans and so on – shaped vaguely to look like a car. Lawrence and Lydia study it for about twelve seconds, pronounce it the best item, then demand to be allowed back to the slope.

'After we've seen a few more things,' says Peter. They groan.

'No, come on,' I say. 'One more floor and then you can.'

We get them to agree to this, only because there are lifts and escalators and they can therefore choose one mode of conveyance each. Peter takes Lawrence and I take Lydia. A few moments after we've separated, the fire alarm goes off. We stop.

'Hang on: it might be a test.'

But it seems not. I clutch Lyd's hand very tightly and we join the flood of people pouring slowly down the stairs.

'Where's Daddy and Lawrence?'

'Don't worry; they'll be down there somewhere.'

I've already decided they're in a small upper gallery dying of smoke inhalation, but we do indeed see them when we emerge.

'That was fun!'

'Is it going to burn down?!'

They do another twenty minutes on the slope, then we go for lunch.

'That was great!'

*

Buoyed by their enthusiasm for – if not Art, then at least the places where other people go to look at it – I decide to take Lydia to the National Gallery. I figure the Impressionists are ideal: lakes, people swimming, ladies in pretty dresses, dancing . . . what's not to like? We're on our way to buy a tutu for £29.95, her reward for not coming into our room for fourteen nights in a row, and it's more or less on the way. Well, if we change trains a couple of times, then get a bus.

'You said we were going to buy a *tutu*!'

'We are. This is only On the Way.'

'Well, I don't want to!'

I steer her determinedly through the doors and up to *La Loge*, Renoir's painting of a woman in a box at the opera. My father taught me that trying to see too much puts people off. There's no need to see every picture in a place; just one room is often enough.

'Hasn't she got a lovely stripey dress?'

'I hate this place!'

And sure enough we last about twelve minutes before, in a state of agitation I've never quite seen before, she goes off into the adjoining gallery, from where I collect her, and we leave.

'Don't ever take me there again!'

'Er, all right. What was it? What didn't you like?'

'You KNOW! *That place!*'

I can't get any more out of her. Later she reveals that one of the guards told her off for sitting on the seat in the middle of the other room – the seat you *are* allowed to sit on – making me feel annoyed and impotent because it's too late to go back, let alone find the right one to get him to repair my daughter's relationship with Renoir and for that matter all the rest of the Impressionists and post-Impressionists. We go home, all tutu'd up but with nowhere, culturally speaking, to go.

Then not long after, we get another chance. Patrick, a parent at school, suggests taking his two and mine to the Victoria and Albert Museum to see 'Touch Me', a hands-on show of modern design.

'There are buttons to press and all that sort of stuff,' he says. It sounds ideal. Also, I still nurse the futile hope that I can somehow ingest a dose of sixteenth-century lutes or some other unchild-friendly display, as we gallop past. Even more futilely, I anticipate a beneficial effect from the company of Patrick himself. The first time we went out with our children, his daughter Ella fell out of a tree and scratched both legs. While I stood there shuddering at the sight of 2 mm of blood, he just picked her up and said, 'You'll be all right.' And of course she was. So I've been hoping to be effortlessly influenced by a parenting style so minimal as to be like one of those transparent Phillippe Starck chairs; you can't see it very well, but it works.

We get to the V&A and to the hands-on exhibition, where they like putting their hands through holes to feel mystery objects such as a model of the Eiffel Tower, and sucking sweets to discover that things inside your mouth feel bigger, particularly if you try to eat twenty all at once. Following the captions, Patrick and I try to escape what the show calls the 'tyranny of vision' by looking away from the children for as long as six or eight seconds, and 'use touch to back up impressions we receive through sight and hearing', when we detect shouting and have to get all four of them off the 'Hug' chair designed for two. The rest of the exhibition emerges unscathed, except possibly for a bunch of stuff like giant spaghetti which hangs from the ceiling in the 'immersive and responsive tactile environment' and is meant to be gently stroked to evoke radio signals, not climbed up.

After about an hour of that, and deploying our sensory powers through our mouths to say 'Stop running' a lot, we go out into the posh new courtyard *with pond*. This has opened recently to tons of gushing write-ups, evidently from the sort of people whose biggest fantasy is to sit in a garden with no plants. With an almost total lack of foliage apart from a few oddly sterile-looking citrus trees in grey pots, there are no surprises, secret vistas, or anything interesting or pleasurable – for any age group – except, of course, for the unfenced circle of *water*. I flop into a chair while the children chase each other round it. It's quite big but shallow, and Lydia immediately shouts, 'Just like Somerset House!'

This is something in retrospect I should have listened to more closely – and might have, I realize afterwards, if I weren't almost asleep as soon as my bum hit the chair. I let my head flop, with one eye semi-trained on the pond, but it's OK because Patrick is watching them.

Some minutes later, I hear raised adult voices and look up to see two quite annoyed museum guards watching all four kids enjoying a paddle. And, due to the Infant Law of Escalation according to which any enjoyable activity will become more enjoyable the more vigorously it's pursued, they are gradually removing their clothes, and in the case of the girls, attempting to wash their hair.

I go over to where Patrick is calmly trying to persuade them to come out – reflecting briefly that behaviour which is infuriatingly ineffectual in a spouse is commendably unflappable in someone else – and bark at Lydia and Lawrence:

'Come out of there, right now!'

I then say to the guards, 'I'm so sorry! I didn't see them go in.'

'Yes, you did,' one of them says, jerking his head in the direction of my chair. I fleetingly consider pushing him in.

'Well, I'm sorry,' I say. 'They thought it was like Somerset House. You know – where they invite children to jump in the fountains. I mean, how are they supposed to know?'

They look at me blankly.

'Is there, for example, a sign?'

They look even more blankly. This is a museum celebrating the best of British design and the decorative arts, so what would it be doing with signs?

We go off with soaking shoes, jeans and hair and drip all over a friendly pizza restaurant, and I decide to leave the whole subject of galleries for at least a decade, or until another parent tells me their seven-year-old is an active Friend of the Royal Academy, and I feel compelled to take us all back.

13 Listen With Mother

The first sound a baby hears is supposed to be his mother's heartbeat. I say supposed to be, because in my case it was almost certainly my digestion. But whatever the first sound was, I was damned if the second one was going to be 'The Wheels on the Bus'.

People are totally divided about 'The Wheels on the Bus'. It's like Israel; there is no middle ground.

When we'd just moved into this pleasant little corner of South London, Lawrence was two, and Lydia one, and apart from Peter's sister, whose children were in their twenties, I knew no one at all. I also knew that the easiest way to meet other mothers, or at least to break up the day, was by going to a playgroup. But even without advance warning of the Singing, it was a difficult prospect for me. Anything that contains the word Group, or that might be an actual Group, or in any way Group-*like*, is something I can't join. I get this sensation of disappearing, like a sort of drowning, and I just can't stand it. The only time I've ever overcome this was when I had group therapy, and I only managed that because (a) the leader was fantastic, (b) everyone in the group was fantastic, and (c) they were completely used to people being terrified of quite normal things, like love. So when I said, 'I hate groups, really hate them', no one thought it was weird.

Therefore when I discovered there was a playgroup opposite my house, I had mixed feelings. On the one hand, I had an opportunity to alleviate the loneliness of five days a week spent alone with a one- and a two-year-old. But on the other hand, I was likely to end up leaving after ten minutes with a panic attack. And no amount of coffee and biscuits, even M&S Extremely Chocolatey ones – which they never have at these things anyway – could alleviate *that*.

Alert readers of my previous book may remember that I'd already had a bad experience at a thing called *Tick Tock* where the leader dressed up as the Farmer's Wife and ran around with a cardboard axe after children who'd obligingly dressed up as mice. Still, I forced myself.

I brought a magazine, which I kept in my hand the whole time to avoid sitting alone with no one to talk to. I chose *The Economist*, which I don't understand a word of, but Peter had a copy and I thought it would help keep people away. If I'd got a normal magazine there was a danger someone might speak to me, which I dreaded about as much as no one speaking to me.

It was all fine until the end. There was a little slide which Lydia liked, so I could steer her down it without having to talk to anyone, and Lawrence concentrated pretty much on the tricycles – all of them at once, including other people's – leaving me free to avoid all contact with the other Grown-ups, who were chatting to each other in that way that people do in Groups where you're new and don't know anyone and are suddenly being very nice to your kids because they at least protect you from contact with anyone else. Mind you, if it weren't for the kids you wouldn't have to be there in the first place, but let's not, as they say, Go There.

Everything was fine until it was time to put the toys away, which I did helpfully along with the others. Then someone said, 'Right, let's all sit down!' or something like that, and suddenly I found myself, with the children, sitting on the floor. And the next thing I knew, someone had got out *a guitar*.

The rest of it I suppose I must have suppressed to some extent, because I remember very little between hearing strangled squeaking sounds coming out of my mouth, and getting in my front door. I know I stayed till the end, because if there's one thing more hideously appalling than being in a Group and Singing, it's leaving in the middle with everyone staring disapprovingly. If you remember poor Laura in *The Glass Menagerie*, explaining to her mother why she's quit typing school and has only been pretending to go, the thing that made it impossible for her was everyone watching while she dragged up the aisle to her desk with her bad leg. Honey, I am *with you*. And as the alternative is staying at home with a mother who tries to rope in Gentlemen Callers and tell them what a great cook her daughter is, thus constantly sabotaging her chances, you can see why she pretends to keep going.

The other reason I stuck it out that day is the knowledge that it's impossible, once you have children, to make a Quick Exit. Every time I've wanted to leave Peter, and there have been several, I've been stopped in my tracks by the realization that I will have to either (a) get them out of bed and put them in the car to God knows where, having packed their toothbrushes, clean pants, paper and coloured pencils – Lydia might one day forgive me for leaving her father, but *never* for leaving her without drawing materials – or (b) leave them behind. So as I can't face organizing (a), and I can't deal mentally with (b), bang goes the Escape every time. Even from a room in a church hall, it cannot be done. I knew where their coats were, but just to get them through the double swing doors and into the pushchair would have slowed me down irrevocably. And when that happens, you've Lost the Moment. Consider Mr Pooter in *The Diary of a Nobody*, after a row with his son: '*I left the room with silent dignity, but caught my foot in the mat.*'

So we stayed, and warbled 'The Wheels on the Bus', and several other atrocities, to the strumming of the woman on the guitar and our own clapping. And never went there again.

Our quest from then on, as I saw it, was to avoid all situations which might include, or lead to the inclusion of, Children's Music. And indeed, bad singing, bad lyrics and communal vocal coercion of any kind. Admittedly, it was more my quest than Peter's. He's always thought I was strange in having *any* taste in music at all, nursing as he does a bizarre conviction that women don't have preferences in this area. (Where do men get this from? Nick Hornby novels? I identified with Rob in *High Fidelity*, so there.) He believes it's another reason I'm part bloke. But since that's *so* weird as to defy analysis, I won't waste your time debunking it. Mind you, we used to say men couldn't taste orange Smarties. The point is, women don't listen to music in a boring, *Ten Best Guitar Solos* kind of way, that's all. They just listen to it. End of argument.

But one thing he *did* understand, and very well, was what lack of exposure to decent music can do to the human spirit. He'd travelled in the Eastern Bloc; he'd been to Albania. When Khrushchev saw the swimming pools of California and said, *'Now I see why Communism has failed'*, he'd have done well to give Enver Hoxha a call and say, *'Forget it, mate: it's a lost cause. They'll be swimming the Straits of Otranto in shoals just to hear four bars of The Shirelles.'*

And just as there was a woman on that trip to Albania who smuggled in tiny Bibles sewn into the hem of her skirt, we see it as our mission not just to vaccinate our own children against oral pollution of the order of 'The Wheels on the Bus', but if at all possible, to save others too.

You think I'm overstating the case? Practically from the moment they draw breath, our children are exposed to Crap. Specially commissioned, appalling 'sub-music' infiltrates impressionable young ears from a frightening variety of sources. School, to our horror, turned out to be one.

'Miss Twinkle wasn't there today, Mummy.'

'So what did you do?'

'Watched a video . . .'

Parents *must* be vigilant. There is Drivel out there, being inflicted on innocent children who can't protect themselves. And it's coming through the wires into your home. Wake up! And do something about it before it's too late.

The first step is to surreptitiously remove the offending material to the charity box, and introduce more suitable fare in its place. Your own television you can at least switch off before something dodgy comes on – make sure you keep the TV listings to hand. As I mentioned in *Confessions of a Bad Mother*, we 'lost' several early videos including *Bob the Builder* and *Titch* and later on, grew even more adept at finding Woolworths and co 'sold out' of certain titles even before they'd come on the market.

The next stage is to get them used to the decent stuff. *Sergeant Pepper* was an early favourite, swiftly followed by *The Best of Burt Bacharach*, the soundtrack of *The Graduate* and *Hair*. Yes, there was a teeny problem with the 'rude words' track on that last one, but we dealt with that by skipping over it and, above all, by *not panicking*. Last year I bought Lydia *The Very Best of T-Rex* and we've never looked back.

Well, no: we have. Because, of course, that's only half the story. When they started going to play at other children's houses, the onslaught of malign influences on their aesthetic development was let loose: *Fimbles*, *Tweenies*, *Balamory* ... there was no telling where it might end.

My advice to concerned parents is this. If other parents ask, when inviting yours round to play, if there's anything they don't like, they're liable to be confused by the answer, 'Very annoying, banal music'. And no one wants to be the parent of the kid who can't go anywhere because they're allergic to bad taste. They can feel like a freak, even end up with no friends. And then they'll have to hang around you all the time, so you don't want *that*. The trouble is, when the damage is done early, it's far harder to repair. All you can do is calmly explain why it's OK to listen to that stuff at school or other people's houses if they have to, but you don't want it going on at home.

Looking back on that aspect of my own upbringing, my parents had no truck with crap music. They had great taste, God bless them. Of course, until we had children and he saw the value of it, Peter always used my exposure to Hip Sounds as a stick to beat me with. It was hilarious enough that I grew up in *Bloomsbury*. My parents actually only had unorthodox and trendy music in the flat. That was 'normal' to them. Well, *sorry*, Mr Normal, but they liked it. And so did we. Claire and

I spent many happy hours leaping round the sitting room in nothing but wisps of coloured net to *Carmina Burana*, *Black Orpheus*, 'The More I See You' by Chris Montez and Nina Simone's classic album *I Put a Spell on You*. Quite often, friends came round and leapt too. Inevitably, there were parents who failed to see this as a Good Thing. The two daughters of the couple who kept the corner shop were banned from playing with us after we spent the afternoon together dancing wildly to 'Gimme Some', Simone's rhythmically irresistible sex anthem, dressed only in beads.

Now we come to the part where my brilliant Music Policy goes wrong. I decide to rent *Saturday Night Fever*. In 1978 this was the BIG movie. Well, for white people. The dancing was terrible, but hey, I was seventeen, I saw it with my boyfriend and afterwards we went to a club where the DJ dedicated a record to me because I had the same name as the main girl in the film. That summer I went to Corfu with three friends on my first holiday without my parents, and it was there too: 'Night Fever', 'You Should Be Dancing' and 'More Than a Woman'. We danced to it every night. It was our first Summer of Freedom. So I think, yeah! Nostalgia! And by a handy coincidence, Lydia LOVES John Travolta. *Grease* is her all-time favourite, and I figure Lawrence will identify with the happy-go-lucky gang of mates element, if not entirely the blue-collar Brooklyn posturing. Unfortunately, I have slightly misremembered it.

It opens with Travolta as Tony Manero walking down a street in Brooklyn with hair like Nancy Reagan and a truly appalling short leather jacket. Not a good start. He works in a hardware store. OK . . . He lives with his family . . . They have dinner – oh my God, the dialogue and direction are terrible. It's like Woody Allen's parody of his own family in *Radio Days*, except without the rhythm, accuracy or humour. They sound exactly, in fact, like my family. Apart from we're not Italian, but otherwise . . .

This is Tony Manero with his friends:

'*What the fuck – you fuck—*'

'Mummy! They're saying fuck!'

I don't remember this. The swearing is relentless. It makes *Taxi Driver* sound like *Mary Poppins*. There's even the N-word. Only once, thank God.

'Children, that's a very, very bad word for black people that you must never, *ever—*'

'Shut up, Mummy! We're missing it!'

Then there's the treatment of women. They all kiss Tony and want to dance with him, and he treats them like crap. The film proceeds. He dances a bit, swears and goes to the hardware store and sells paint. Behind me, Lydia is trying on a cheongsam dress from some friends of Peter's that she wants to wear to school for Chinese New Year, which makes her look even more beautiful. She reclines along the back of the new Ikea armchair – the one with no cover because her father and I cannot agree on the colour, pattern or style – looking like a goddess. She is seven. On the screen, Tony's girlfriend, having been thrown over for his new dancing partner, is on the rebound, having sex with his friends, in turn, in the back of the car. And by the end of the first one, she is crying. Ah. Um, Lydia . . .

'It's like she's being tortured!'

Lydia isn't so much distressed as baffled.

'Yes. Well, you see . . . she's having sex with him, which she – er, thought she wanted to, but she doesn't really. Promise me you'll never – oh, God . . .' Another bloke gets in the back and has a go, which she *definitely* doesn't want. Eventually she gets out of the car, weeping, and staggers about on the bridge.

Tony then calls her a Very Bad Word.

'Mummy, what's a cunt?'

'Er . . .'

I have now officially wrecked my children's innocence. I just want to die. I mean, this just isn't the film as I remember it. How have I involuntarily censored it in my memory? I have no idea. But I've got to defend myself somehow; I see Peter coming in.

Shit. I have to get him out of here, though if he starts anything, I can remind him of the Ian McEwan novel he recommended to me when we first lived together, in which a woman is permanently disabled by her husband's sexual 'technique'. We almost split up over it. That's *much* worse than John Travolta saying cunt. Hmm. Can I head him off at the pass, before he discovers that, thanks to my faulty memory – filtered through the abnormally large, rose-tinted shades of the seventies – his children are hearing the C- and N-words, and watching date rape? No. If I start apologiz-ing now for all the things I've accused him of in the last seventeen years that I've done myself, we could be here all—

'Well, Mummy?'

'Ooh. Erm. I'll tell you when – well, I can't explain now because we'll miss the film. Oh, hello, darling! You wouldn't get me another drink, would you? Look, they're near the edge of the bridge again. Um, I think something bad might be about to happen. Promise me you won't ever do this.'

I'm pretty sure someone is going to fall off; yes, I do remember that much. Tony is trying to comfort the girl. She's still teetering about, sobbing and snuffling, so we're meant to think it's she who's going to fall off, but it's his mate, the one who's got his girlfriend pregnant and doesn't want to marry her. He's dancing about on the edge, in an I'm-about-to-fall-off-but-I-don't-know-it-even-though-it's-really-obvious kind of way. There's a brief build-up, done very badly because the film has no sense of pace, and suddenly he's in the water, a long way down. Lydia runs round to the other side of the glass doors that divide the sitting room, so she can see the screen, but at a remove.

'You shouldn't have let me see that, Mummy.'

'Right. Right. Yes. Good point.'

What is it Homer says one time? *'Look, why don't we forget about Bart and Lisa and just concentrate on the other one?'* If only I had a third child I could bring up with a clean slate. I try to comfort myself with the thought that the dropping of uppers, downers and 'ludes seems to have passed them by, but it's a small mercy. So I focus on my fear that Lawrence will go driving around with his rich, public school friends – maybe we should move him to a state school where they'll be less able to afford cars – and fall off bridges for a thrill on a Saturday night.

Peter returns with my drink, and I persuade him to take Lydia up to do her teeth. That way I can postpone having to explain myself, and have to just hope that she doesn't drop me in it from too great a height.

'Lawrence,' I say in my Sensible Voice. 'Promise me,

if you're ever with some guys and they're, you know, drinking and falling off things, you won't join in. *Please?*'

If there's one good thing that can come out of this experience, it'll be my repackaging of SNF as a Public Information Film.

'Don't worry, Mum. I'll probably just chat and go for pizzas. I won't drink, and I won't do that.'

He has made the connection between the bottles they've been swigging from and their bravado – well, possibly. But the main thing is, he's given me his solemn promise that he will never go out in a white suit with huge lapels, with hair like Nancy Reagan, and fall off the Brooklyn Bridge. So that's good. And what's more, he won't do it in a badly touched-up 1963 Chevy Impala which is doubly good, because, that being the year they got rid of the fins and other fun styling, it was a hideous car.

So I go to bed with the hope that my children will at least have been put off drinking, getting into cars with people, getting out of cars on bridges, and overacting. And *Saturday Night Fever* may yet turn out to have been of benefit after all. Which is a relief, because you know what's the weirdest thing of all? It doesn't even contain that much dancing.

14 A Time to Eat Cakes

Considering how shocked I was the first time I saw my parents cry, you'd think I'd make more effort not to myself. One of the things that's clearly surprised the children about me is my terrible soppiness, a total lack of *backbone* in the face of anything sad. Or anything happy. Or just – anything. I cry at funerals, weddings, of course, christenings, carol services, documentaries, feature films, novels, adverts and Disney films I don't even like. *The Fox and the Hound*, a cartoon mired in a sentimental anthropomorphism viscous even by Walt's own standards, had me snuffling while even Lydia was dry-eyed.

'It's all right, Mummy: it's only a video,' she soothed.

I cry at *Ben-Hur, The Ten Commandments* or any Hollywood epic with Charlton Heston and/or Jesus in it, where people die for noble causes, die with a beatific smile, or, in the case of Jennifer Jones in *The Song of Bernadette*, die with a beatific smile and a rotting leg.

And whatever the content, I go right off if the backing singers do that 'angelic choir' thing. It doesn't matter what it's about. I also cried at the end of *Cyrano de Bergerac* because – oh dear – I thought it had a happy ending. While everyone was flipping up their seats and making their way to the exits, I was still in my chair, sobbing.

'I thought the guy with the huge nose was going to get the girl!' I blubbed to my mother. He was played by Gerard Depardieu, after all. In Hollywood, he would have. In Hollywood, he *did*. (*Roxanne*, starring Daryl Hannah and Steve Martin.) Bloody French.

Claire says, 'I remember you crying almost uncontrollably at *Dumbo* in the cinema when Dad took us. You were quite old – maybe ten or so – and I was embarrassed because a man looked round.'

'Oh, bloody hell.'

'But then one time Lydia and Lawrence were watching it on video when I was there, and I had to leave the room at the bit when they lock up the mother because I couldn't bear it. Needless to say, they were fine!'

Um, I am starting to cry as I type this bit, because I've just remembered the bit where she puts her trunk out of the prison window, and . . .

BLUB!

Bloody Walt Disney. He's got a lot to answer for.

Claire adds, 'Would you like to know all the other things that make me cry?'

'What, there's more?'

'Weddings, babies, children, people being happy, people being unhappy, people being scared to say they love someone and missing their chance, people getting old, *Brat Camp*, baby clothes, every episode of *Bleak House*, almost all drama. Every episode of *ER*, even if there aren't any shot children in it.'

'*Brat Camp*?'

'Yes, because it's just so moving when you see those stroppy teenagers changing, their faces becoming clearer...'

'Someone told me they've been known to feel sorry for a single apple in a bowl.'

'Oh no!'

'Awful, isn't it?'

But then I remember Lydia, watching television one day and wanting something to eat.

'You can have a muffin,' I'd said, 'but not in there.'

'I won't spill any.'

'Whatever. I don't want it on the carpet.'

She looked wistfully in the direction of the counter.

'I feel sorry for the muffin.'

'Don't be,' I said. 'The muffin doesn't want to watch *Tom and Jerry*. It's a cake. Cakes don't get lonely, they get eaten: that's their job.'

But deep down, I saw what she meant.

My mother said, 'You fool! She just wanted the cake.'

But she doesn't realize. Not being the sentimental type given to snuffling over single pieces of fruit, she sees only an ulterior motive. But I know that such pointlessly tragic feelings are not unique. The Mitford sisters used to make each other burst into tears by reciting a made-up poem about a match.

I mention this to my friend Lucy, who claims to trump us all.

'I cry at everything,' she insists. 'Those *Little Bear* books. I blame *Bambi*.' After viewing that notorious animation, she couldn't stop herself blubbing at the slightest thing. 'I was quite a happy child before that.'

'They say it starts when you get pregnant.'

'That's bollocks.'

'Well, I know, because when I was four, there was this bit they added at the end of the school nativity play, when everyone sings 'Oh Come All Ye Faithful' and the Rich and Poor Children join hands. I was a Poor Child. And I just sobbed.'

'That *is* pathetic.' She looks at me in a new light.

'It was in a real church,' I explain. 'With the organ going full blast.'

'Yeah, but it's the parents who are meant to cry at these things, not the kids.'

'I know. Lydia's got this one about a mermaid – *Can You Catch a Mermaid?*, that's it – about this girl who lives with just her dad and's got no one to play with. She finds a mermaid and sort of tricks her into staying because she's so lonely, and at the end has to do the right thing and let her go back to the sea, and she misses her so much . . .'

But here I have to stop because I am getting a lump in my throat. When I read it out, it always ends with Lydia frowning over the bedcovers at me, disbelieving the evidence that her supposedly Grown-up mother can't get to the end of a picture book without dissolving into tears. And that's having read it before. I suppose it's like *Casablanca*: the minute she says, 'Play it, Sam,' you're a goner. It doesn't matter how many times you hear it. But children's books, though! Come on.

'I know!' Lucy's worst embarrassment was in public, at Milo's school.

'I had to read to the class, and it was *The Happy Prince*, which is just So Sad. The words were just swimming about. I couldn't even see.'

'What's the story of *The Happy Prince*?' I ask, rashly.

'I don't think I've ever read it.' She pours us another beer, so we are sitting comfortably, and begins.

By the end we are both weeping. Lawrence and Milo come in to see if dinner's ready yet.

'What's going on?'

'Has someone died?'

'No, no – we're fine.'

'We were just enjoying a story.'

They look at each other, shake their heads and go back to *Adventure Quest*.

Bizarrely, when something *really* sad happens, I don't go to pieces at all.

Lydia sometimes plays Orphans with her friends.

'How did your parents die?' I ask.

'In a fire!' she trills, 'like in *Lemony Snicket*.'

I found that story disturbing. When we saw the film, the idea of children being handed into the charge of any character played by Jim Carrey made it really quite difficult to watch.

In the books of my childhood, being an orphan was fun. Parentless children – such as the Fossil sisters in *Ballet Shoes*, had wonderful adventures with benefactors, inheritances and did lots of *pliés*, as opposed to being taken into care and learning how to smoke dope. They were masters of their own fates. And despite being emotionally buffeted by our parents' divorce when I was five, my sister and I were never troubled by the thought of losing them altogether.

'Mummy, when you die, can we have your white lace blouse and purple diamond earrings?' we would inquire regularly. And she would reply, 'Of course!'

I've got no time for the euphemisms people use on children about death. I'm not interested in Heaven, unless it takes place in a restaurant, and telling them so-and-so has 'gone to sleep' is surely a recipe for lifelong insomnia. Anyhow, it insults their intelligence. Families with pets tell me they're very useful for getting kids 'used to the idea'. In other words, they bring a hamster, kitten or puppy into the house primarily so they can watch them die. But I still think, even for Key Stage 1 Mortality, wet straw, slimey tanks, constant scrabbling sounds or, God forbid, the smell of cat food, is too high a price to pay. So I just cut out the middle cat and give it to them straight.

Lawrence's first experience of death was Peter's Aunt Doreen, aged ninety-five, when he was three. When we told him, he asked, 'When you die, do you come alive again?'

And I said, 'I don't think so, no. Some people think it's not the end, but I do.'

He became upset for a few minutes, saying, 'I don't want to die!' And then you could see him sort of processing it, and he knew that she wasn't coming back. The only confusion that arose about her whereabouts was while she was still alive, as the home was in Crystal Palace. 'Aunty lives at the Huge Aerial,' he would say, since for some of us, mortality is less of a challenge than geography.

I got to see death from Lawrence's current perspective at age eight, following the death of Peter's much older cousin. The funeral was held at the university where he taught, and I asked Lawrence what he liked best.

'The coloured windows,' he said, which was fair enough. The circular Meeting House had – not stained glass, but rows of small windows in groups of plain colours: reds, blues, greens and so on.

'Anything you weren't sure about?'

'Cakes! We were literally *celebrating*.'

To paraphrase Ecclesiastes, there's a Time to Eat Cakes, and, according to him, this wasn't it – although he did fight his disapproval sufficiently to manage three. He had a point. Why, when we've just lost someone, do we have a party? It's not just the comforting property of tea, although I wouldn't underestimate that. The Chaplain had said eating and drinking together is a vital part of the ceremony. And of course we're sharing memories, and reasons why the dead person was so loved. But, now I see it through eight-year-old eyes, it does seem strange. And this particular occasion was even more incongruous, to me anyway, as the first thing the Chaplain did when we came out was to tell me a Jewish joke. So, having been crying five minutes before, I was now roaring with laughter. We both got some Looks.

And here's the funny thing. He told me the joke because his own father had recently died, not long after discovering he was Jewish. And afterwards I thought – even though I don't believe in these things – that my father sent me that joke. I won't tell the children that, though; they'd know it was one of those silly things Grown-ups invent because they can't handle life's harsh truths.

15 Burn Him Off, Pegasus!

Recently I was looking through the paper and came across a competition: *Win a Film Star Lifestyle for a Year!* There were loads of prizes: a posh handbag by someone I'd never heard of, a year's supply of some magical death-defying cream, a year's supply of oakmoss & vetiver 'designer' candles, a year's supply of something described as a 'cult lip gloss', a year's subscription to a glossy magazine, a holiday in Mauritius and a truly hideous diamond ring. I read through them again and realized, to my surprise, that I didn't want them. I was shocked. It was like going into a restaurant and suddenly not wanting chips. I quite fancied the holiday, but not enough to bother to collect the tokens. And anyway, it was only for two. *What's happening to meee?* A terrible thought occurred. My fantasies have – dried up. Or have they just changed?

New parents dream only of sleep. In the first few days they think they can handle it because the baby is bound to start sleeping through any day now, and by the end of the first month, they'll sell their own mothers for four uninterrupted hours. Once the children are toddling, dreams of romantic weekends with long dinners have shrunk to a meal, anywhere, served by someone else. A takeaway counts, as long as someone else gets it out of the box.

My own personal desires have gone from winning the Academy Award for Best Screenplay, to not having to unwrap any more mouldy games kit. As for anything erotic, forget it, though while I'm on the subject let's blow the lid off one myth about women. The reason a lot of them don't want sex any more isn't because of childbirth; it's because their husbands are boring, balding and fat. Female Sexual Dysfunction? Take a look in the mirror, blobby!

I once saw a survey which revealed that given a choice of treats, most women would rather have a cleaner than spend more time with their husbands. When I tell Peter, he says, 'That's because they're not married to me.'

Even so, men aren't as one-dimensional as we've been led to believe. Sure, they start off thinking about sex every 2.1 seconds, but they too change with age. As he gazes at you across the lino, the father of your children may not be thinking: *I don't care if you're wearing frayed leggings and a T-shirt like a whale's scrotum: I still want to fuck you.* No. That intense, smouldering look actually says: *I want to be speeding along the Riviera in a BMW M5 making my friends sick with envy, not watching you lean over your stomach to clip your toenails into the bin.*

Because, let's be honest, when you have to pick your way through cheesy baby bottles, chairs with jam on and a bed full of biscuit crumbs just to find a clean shirt, the bachelor's life with its lone pizza in the fridge can fill you with misty-eyed longing. Peter insists he's way past all that, but he's not. When he was walking the children back from the park one Sunday at 10 a.m. – yes, *back* from the park at 10 a.m. – he says he saw people reading their papers over coffee and croissants outside the café, and his eyes positively watered as he described the scene. He then told every single person who phoned or visited us for the rest of the year.

Sex therapists sometimes suggest sharing your fantasies. And we already have one in common: the desire to sit down in front of the telly one night without having to rebuild the furniture because it's all been turned into a den. If the living room were suddenly free of toys, paper, takeaway menus and Geomag, we'd both cry out in simultaneous ecstasy.

But there are things he likes to do to me which I try

to resist. I've told him the whole point of fantasies is that they stay in your head, but he says he can't help it.

Sometimes, when I'm in the bathroom at night, I can see him eyeing me up, harbouring unspeakable thoughts. He hovers in the doorway and I can see it on his face. He's scrutinizing my skin for spots. If he thinks he's found one, a look of pleasure crosses his face because he wants to squeeze it.

'You have something on your chin,' he says.

'No, I haven't.'

He advances.

'Get off.'

He says, 'You say you don't want it, but you do.'

He comes nearer, hands raised, like a surgeon. We struggle. And sometimes, because in marriage you have to consider a man's needs, I give in.

My own, rather tragic *need*, if that's the right word, is to flirt with other men. And one place in which I can maintain the delusion of being irresistible is in the car. Cars are good for being mysterious. It's probably why so many men use them as pretend invisible booths to pick their noses in. My sister and I used to kneel on the back seat of Dad's Austin 1100 and aim death rays at the people behind. Now, with a bit of power under my foot, I burn men off at the lights.

I got into this very immature habit in Dubai, where I lived briefly twenty years ago with a nice man called Des. He had a totally dull company Nissan but the engine was a decent size, and for me a big step up from the last car I'd driven, my mum's Datsun Cherry, in which I was once stopped by the police for driving too slowly. Though women were allowed to drive, there weren't that many of them on the roads. So while the man in the lane next to me was gawping, I'd hit the gas and whizz off. Well, until they built all those islands in the shape of the world, you had to make your own fun.

I blame Roger Moore and Tony Curtis. My sister and I were great devotees of *The Persuaders*, and although at ten we had no idea of the difference between a 1969 Ferrari Dino, an Aston Martin DBS and a tractor, somehow the idea of cars as sexy caught on. Then came *American Graffiti*, and one sight of Harrison Ford and Paul Le Mat revving and curling their lips at each other was enough to get me addicted for good. The fact that Harrison's character ends up climbing injured from his upside-down Chevy Hot Rod, and Le Mat's career subsequently nosedived, made no odds.

I continued to do it when Peter got a black company BMW, which was ideal except for the slight misunderstanding over the choice of seat colour: 'buttermilk' on the card should really have said 'egg yolk'. Still, I was able to get really into my stride with the silver Alfa 156, a car that assuaged my desire for a Jaguar XK120 or even a TVR for two very good reasons. One: when we first got it, it had just come on the market, so men kept stopping to ask me about it. I could bang on about the 24-valve V6 engine, which was just brilliant. Mind you, having said that, I always had to drive away fairly quickly because that was all I knew:

Exterior. Day. Petrol Station.

'See you've got the new 156.'

'Yeah! It's great.'

'My wife wants the BMW, but I'm considering this instead. Is it the V6?'

'Yeah.'

'How does it handle?'

'Fantastic. It's really – *responsive*. We wouldn't go back to the BMW now.'

'Really? Right. The seats are quite bright, aren't they?'

'Yeah. They were supposed to be a sort of blue-grey, but . . .'

'Well, thanks anyway. Bye.'

And two: it has great door handles. Actually, that's why we chose it.

Now, as I see Forty speeding away from me on the wrong side of life's dual carriageway, I know that not every man who happens to look in my direction at the lights wants to sleep with me – or, quite possibly, none of them. They don't even want my car, since it is now eight years old and has bits of Babybel in the creases of the seats. If they're thinking anything, my guess is it's more along the lines of, *I wish I was taller, I should have slept with more women before I got married/became old and repulsive* or: *I wish this was a DB9.*

And because we've had children, we must inevitably turn our attention away from our fantasies and in the direction of theirs. Lawrence, for example, has already passed the point where he'll admit to wanting to be a secret agent. We've read *Silverfin* and *Bloodstorm* featuring the young James Bond, and he is now reading the five books about Alex Rider, who embarks on a career with MI5, aged fourteen. But if I say, 'Hey, Lawrence: if we were Secret Agents we could drive about shooting baddies all the time!' he's fairly likely to answer, 'That's a bit silly, Mum, don't you think?'

And he's not even nine. It reminds me of when, still quite little, in a sandpit somewhere, he served me a pretend meal.

'Mmm!' I said. 'It's chicken, isn't it?'

'No, Mummy,' he said, 'it's sand.'

Anyhow, this is a bit from Alex Rider's first adventure, *Stormbreaker*:

'There was the roar of an engine and then a billowing cloud of red fire exploded over the grass. One of the riders was carrying a flame thrower ... Choking, his face streaked with dirt and sweat, he clambered out of the ditch and ran blindly forward. He had no idea where he was going any more.'

I have a bit more difficulty identifying with Lydia's heroes.

Lydia is in the throes of full-blown Animal Magic. She becomes, intermittently, a pony, or a kitten, or a rabbit, or a lion cub. But the other night I came in to turn out the light and she was feverishly tracing the illustrations in Usborne's *Greek Myths*. We'd run out of tracing paper so she was using baking parchment. Bits of it were flying everywhere. The place was covered with pictures of Pegasus. I thought that was particular to her, and the cultural superiority of our household with the *Greek Myths*, but that was before I discovered how many books there are on the market about horses who can fly.

Of the five series of books she's currently keen on, three are about ponies and two of those spend a fair bit of their time airborne. There's Twilight in *My Secret Unicorn*, *My Magical Pony* and *Sheltie*, the first two featuring winged equine protagonists with highly developed forensic skills. *My Magical Pony* books have plots about skullduggery at the stables: *'A gang of horse thieves steal ponies from Krista's stables and she feels she's to blame! Shining Star is on hand to help, but they find the ponies trapped at the edge of a dangerous cliff.'* I particularly like 'dangerous cliff'.

Shining Star appears in a cloud of glitter dust, beating his giant wings to bear heroine Krista off to her next adventure, whereas Twilight is the mono-horned alter ego of a normal pony who can be summoned by a spell. His stories are a bit less Blytonesque than Shining Star's and more prepubescent. In *Flying High* he and heroine Lauren help her friend Jessica who's run away from home. And in *Dreams Come True* they help pony Shadow overcome his phobia of jumps by taking him back to his childhood as a foal when he banged his leg, in what must be the only Recovered Memory session ever facilitated by one quadruped for another. Poor old Sheltie isn't magic, but proves popular nonetheless. His USP, basically, is that he is small – but also plucky:

'Help, Sheltie! Help!' cried Emma.

Sheltie was quick to act. The moment he saw Emma disappear through the hole in the ice he raced to her rescue.

Yes, he has developed opposable thumbs. Actually, he leaps into the icy depths so that Emma can grab his mane, caring nothing for his own safety. He has a less community-spirited brother, though, called Shirtie, whom I've invented as a Brechtian alienation technique to stop myself getting sucked in:

Sheltie pawed the ground urgently.

'Shirtie! Come quickly! Snobby Alice Parker and Silver Lad are stuck on the narrow cliff path!'

'Piss off,' said Shirtie. 'Can't you see I'm reading the racing results?'

'But we need to get help!' Sheltie whinnied.

'Get a life!' snorted Shirtie, as he tossed his chestnut mane before giving him a good kicking.

Collect these thrilling titles: *Shirtie at the Track, Shirtie and the Grass, Shirtie Goes for Broke, Shirtie and the Lap Dancer* and *Shirtie in the Nick*. The final one in the series will be *Shirtie and the Knacker's Yard*.

But I mustn't grumble. One term, both children in succession came home with *Kittens in the Kitchen* as their reading book. It concerned a family who acquire some kittens, I can't remember how, and spend the entire book trying to get rid of them – I mean, find them a good home. The major plot point of Act Two is when the little girl thinks of putting an ad in the newsagent's window. One night when Peter was hearing them read, I found him slumped against the wall in a kind of catatonic trance. Mind you, they both loved it.

So, we know that Lawrence is clear that he isn't Alex Rider, boy secret agent, or the Young James Bond.

But can Lydia see the line between real and imaginary? One day I take her to the Bead Shop, a dazzling Aladdin's Cave of glass and metal shapes, hearts, flowers, fish and animals to thread on things, and afterwards we go to a café for lunch. Squeezing through to get to our table I can hear her saying to people, 'Um, excuse me . . .' And: 'Could you move in a little? Thank you!' One or two of the other diners look baffled, as am I. She isn't getting them to make space for me – I'm not *that* big – and she has bags of room.

'What are you making room for?' I ask finally.

'Little Star!' she says, as if it's obvious. 'My invisible pony.'

Right . . .

When we go to the loo, he has to come with us on his lead. It's a tight squeeze, because most cubicles aren't designed for three and I have to get a bit snappy with her for refusing to shut the door.

I suppose one of the reasons children are generally happier than adults – apart from not having to pay for anything – is that they can experience their real and fantasy worlds as closer together than ours. (There are adults like this too: they're called psychopaths.) I'm quite happy with that. I just have one concern, which is that Lydia will find out we live near a stables. Whenever we drive along that bit of the road I distract her with some pointless observation – 'Look, Lyd! A magpie!' – so she looks the other way. Other than that, all I can do is keep making it clear, if she really is in the early stage of that phase, that we lack the two attributes essential for pony-owning parents: the belief that a green quilted waistcoat is a fashion must-have, and a spare £2,000 a month in the bank to spend on hay. And if we escape that, what's next? Real boys. So for now, I'm all in favour of Twilight and Little Star. They never let you down. They don't even need mucking out.

16 What Do You Call Yours?

A friend of my sister's once told me, years before I even contemplated children, her Most Embarrassing Moment. She was a zoologist, and therefore not easily provoked to blushes. However, she was when she was at the Post Office with her daughter Lucy, aged three at the time. She asked a woman in the queue beside them: 'Are you a Grown-up?'

And the woman said, clearly thinking, *How Sweet*: 'Yes, I suppose I am . . .!'

And Lucy replied loudly: 'Then you must have hairs on your wee-wee!'

It was the clear diction that did it. No one missed a syllable. And ever since then, I've wondered: *If I had a little girl, what would I tell her It was called?*

As an adult you don't generally have to worry. Your husband/boyfriend/whatever doesn't keep referring to it. You both know where it is, so you don't need to. It's not like in *The Archers*, where people have to keep naming things all the time:

'Oh, hello, Ruth, and isn't that Eddie behind you? Yes, there he is, adjusting his winkle.'

'Aw naw! You can't say winkle! You have to say dangly bottom.'

'Oh, hello, Brian! I didn't see you standing behind the hay pile there.'

I don't have any qualms about telling my kids, at this stage aged five and seven, the Facts of Life. I don't shrink from talking about willies getting hard and going into – well, that's just it. There isn't an equivalent of willy, is there? Nor of 'bollocks', a particular favourite of mine. 'Bum' is unisex, thank God, and a great word. But 'front bottom'? I know that if I leave it too long, outside influences will prevail which could lead to confusion. In fact, it's started already. I was a bit taken aback one day a couple of years ago, when I came in to hear that Lydia, running through the house, had collided with the doorway. Recounting the experience, she said: 'I was like a bull in a vagina shop!'

Imagine the sort of muddle she could get into over her wedding list.

Then I saw something that motivated me further. In an otherwise charming children's book about the Facts of Life, whereas the male character had a willy, the female had *nothing at all*. And I thought: *Hang on a minute, mate* – or whatever the female equivalent is – *hang on, love: we're not blank Down There, you know*. I could feel my feminist hackles rising – almost to the point of getting out my We'Moon Diary from 1994 that contains, among other things, a poem with the line, *'Look between my legs: I am singing.'* Actually, the first time I wrote this I typed, *'Look between my legs: I am* signing', which I suppose would be the version for the deaf.

Anyhow, I thought: *We'd better get on with this.*

My problem is that I've never been able to stand the V-word, so much so that I avoid saying it or, in this instance, typing it. But then, I don't like any of the other words either. We said *wee-wee*, I think, when we were small. But, perhaps due to the absence of any males in the household, it wasn't a big deal. There were always more pressing matters to attend to, such as who had more space in the bath. At my father's place, thank God, it never came up. I had privacy in the bathroom as early as I can remember, except for when he came in to wash my hair and got shampoo in my eyes. And I must have graduated to grown-up language at some point, since I definitely don't remember ruining any erotic moments by saying *wee-wee* to those with whom I was *romantically involved*. It's surprising, really, that I should be so hopeless. My mother is

– forthright. She rang me up not long ago to recommend a programme about word definitions she thought I'd like.

'They had Germaine Greer spraying the word *cunt* on a wall,' she said, as if to confirm its appeal.

'Oh. Jolly good!'

There's something about her unflinchingness that brings out the Joyce Grenfell in me. I come over all euphemistic and net curtainy. And the more pursed-lips I get, the more she Goes For It. Of course, she was probably one of the few people watching who knew its original meaning as *queynte*, or small, pretty thing – and this without having an English degree. But here I am again, Avoiding the Issue.

I say we don't know what to call it. We do have a word, actually. Katarina, former nanny and solver of impossible parenting problems, chose the term *noo-noo*. I just came in one day and there it was. But, as I'm sure any *Teletubbies* viewer is aware, it's already taken. Or was. But Katarina, coming from Slovakia, didn't know that. And we, having avoided most baby telly as quickly as possible, didn't either. *Noo-noo* seemed to do the trick, at least in that it was a word I could bring myself to utter, and Lydia, to whom it mattered the most, liked it fine. Lawrence and Peter too. But now I worry that it won't work in the future. What about when she gets to secondary school? Her friends might laugh at her. It certainly won't take her as far as puberty, which these days apparently starts at eight. So that gives us a year.

While I ponder my dilemma I ask around.

I start with Lucy, who seems to be able to cope with most things I throw at her. She has a boy of eight and a girl of four, and, sure enough, gives me my answer illustrated by a helpful anecdote.

'She wants to say *fanny*, but pronounces it really oddly.'

'How?'

'When we went on holiday last year, and she saw a bidet for the first time, I explained what it was. She went around shouting to the other guests that our room had a "bath for washing your fonny!"'

For some reason this makes me think of someone who can't say 'phone' and says 'phon-ee' – like that Monty Python sketch about a man caught selling a dodgy phrase book to a Hungarian, who wants to say, 'Is this the way to the tube?' but ends up asking complete strangers: 'Can I fondle your buttocks?' And, even more embarrassingly: 'My hovercraft is full of eels.' Wait, I know what it reminds me of – *phonics*.

I mention the F-word to another friend, confessing that I don't like it any more than the V one. And she says that her son – when in 'mixed company' – says *funny*. Actually, that one's not bad.

'Trouble,' says a third friend, Julie. 'Or *front door*.'

'*Trouble?!*'

'Well, I am talking about the older generation,' she admits. 'My mother had a catch-all phrase for the entire region from navel to kneecap – *your underneath*; this delivered in hushed tones with eyes cast downwards and a vague hand-waving.'

She says that a friend of hers worked in a care-home where one of her charges said to her, as she approached to do a blanket bath: 'Mind my *front door!*'

'Dear God!'

This triggers a disconcerting memory I have of someone referring to her *barn doors*, but I've blotted out the provenance. I think, on reflection, I'm more com-fortable with the Yorkshire woman I overheard who referred to *problems under my pinny*.

My friend Judith rings me about something consider-ably less intimate, like meeting for lunch. She has triplets the same age as Lawrence – a boy and two girls.

'While you're on,' I say, 'what do the girls call their – you know?' I am horrendously coy. How I ever wrote for *Cosmopolitan* I don't know.

'*Biff.*'

'What?! As in *Biff and Chip*? Blimey.'

'I don't know where they got it from,' she says. 'Just that one of them said it, and I thought, *Great: they've got their own word for it.*'

'Saving you the bother of worrying about it,' I say. Then I remember the shop.

'Would you believe there's a shop called that, right near where we live? They sell ever so gorgeous children's clothes, and the owner is desperately polite.'

'Maybe she does, and named the shop after it.'

'You're not taking this seriously, are you?'

'Yes I am. Their *dingy* is their *biff-willy.*'

'Their *what*?'

'Their clitoris.'

'Ah, right . . .' Another word I have a slight problem with.

'Because when they play with it, they go "*ding-a-ding-a-ding*".' I glance down – not at that – and find I am holding the phone ever so slightly away.

'So that would be a hard "g", as in "small, inflatable boat", or Dingle, a lovely part of Ireland, as opposed to a soft "g" as in "dingy" – sort of grey and gloomy.'

'So, see you at Carluccio's at twelve, then?' she says.

Two days later I take Lawrence for a haircut. I'm sitting there, flicking through *Closer* magazine, when the mobile goes and it's Bad Mothers Club contributor Jane ringing me, though I've forgotten why.

'*Chuff*, or *chufflet*,' she intones solemnly. Then, just as I'm jotting this down: '*the Pink Hole of Calcutta.*'

'*Pink Hole of Calcutta!* Jesus!'

The bloke doing Lawrence's hair looks round briefly, but doesn't react. Nor does he wince, shriek, or faint when I mumble, '*Min-min* ... Hang on, let me get this down ...' The phrase 'Minja Turtles' comes unavoidably to mind at this point, and I have to shout that down the phone at her too. Still no reaction from the bloke doing Lawrence. Mind you, people tell their hairdressers the most intimate details of their lives, so this is probably the least unsettling thing he's heard this week.

On the way back, I remember that Peter once worked with a guy who used to describe certain people as *minge-meisters*, though whether it was people he *did* like, or *didn't*, I don't know.

Finally I get to my sister, whom I pester with every dilemma although she has only a very small boy at this point and no girls at all. She considers the matter fully.

'I have been known to use the word *regions*,' she confesses.

'*Regions* ...'

'It's *Down There* sort of territory,' she adds unnecessarily, reminding me of the title I wanted for the Bad Mothers Club medical page, were we ever to have had one, which we don't.

'Obviously, that's more for casual occasions,' she adds. 'What's wrong with *noo-noo*, anyway?'

'It's a bit – you know, young.'

'No, it's perfect. You need a euphemism with kids, so that when they shout, *'Have you got a furry noo-noo?'* in the Post Office, you can say they're talking about their pet rabbit.'

'Thanks, that's very useful.'

Honestly, how is she going to cope if she ever has a girl? Still, at least she's worse than me, which is some comfort.

Some time after this conversation, Peter's sister has the children for the night, and we get a Night Off. We choose Brighton, partly so we can go out to dinner with two old friends of his who live there. We ask them to choose the restaurant.

'It's Moroccan,' they tell us.

'Great.'

When we get there it's called *Nou Nou*, and, needless to say, the staff can't see why Peter and I are giggling. Actually Peter's being completely normal and *I'm* giggling. It's his birthday – did I mention that? But all I can do is sit there texting Katarina and collecting handfuls of the free boxes of matches. Eventually I collect myself and ask why the restaurant is so-called.

'It's the name of the owner. His nickname,' explains a waitress.

'Is it? Right. Good!' I stifle myself with more wine.

When we get back I tell the children, but to my disappointment they don't think it's as hilarious as I do. The bizarre possibility occurs to me that they may – just – be starting to grow out of this stage, which poses an intriguing question. When they grow up and leave all this behind, will I have to, too?

17 You Can Be Dead

I've never claimed to understand the male gender, but I've had to conclude I understand women even less. There are so many things they do that I don't see the point of, Grown-up Female things that I can't seem to get the hang of. I spend almost nothing on beauty products, never get my nails done and have never had a facial. And what is this thing about *shoes*?

'Shoes? Don't get me started on *shoes*!'

'Oh, I *know*.'

'Shoes. You wear them on your feet, right?'

I just don't get it.

And the thing I get least of all is women's attitude to food. I mean, surely the whole advantage – OK, one of the advantages – of not being a child any more is being able to eat what you like.

Very occasionally, and luckily not often, I get taken to some party where the men are all shapes and sizes – tall, short, warty, whatever – but the women are like this Javanese puppet my mother used to have on the wall. They wear dolls' versions of adult clothes, totter along in tiny, high shoes and have no tits. For them, a pornographic experience is a bakery. And if, God forbid, you have to eat lunch with one of them, it's a miserable experience because the biggest thing they pick up is the menu. Plus there's the spin-off effect they have of making anyone with a normal appetite feel like the Hulk:

ME: It all looks YUMMY!

STICK INSECT: What are you having?

ME: I dunno. Why?

I say this deliberately, because I know stick insects can't order unilaterally, in case they accidentally eat three calories more than you. So I wait. But then I get hungry, so I always weaken first and say what I want anyway.

STICK INSECT: What's in the fish? [A woman I had lunch with once did actually say this.]

WAITER: Fish.

SI: What's it like?

WAITER [sighing]: It's fish.

ME: I'll have the duck in orange and brandy sauce with sauté potatoes and beans. Ooh, and a glass of red wine.

SI: I'll have the rocket and pine nut salad.

[*Exit waiter*]

SI: How many calories d'you think there are in pine nuts?

We then have to waste £3 that could have gone on pudding, buying a bottle of water. So what I want to know, while I sit there troughing like Mike Tyson, is: what is so damn feminine about being on hunger strike? It's not as though they even use it to make a point.

When I look at the Sunday papers or read a magazine, I wonder if I'm living on the same planet as everyone else. If aliens landed in WH Smith's – actually, come to think of it, they probably already have. That would explain it – they would conclude there are Two species of human in the Western Hemisphere: the sweaty, slightly bulging mortals who burp and fart and as they age deteriorate quite horribly, and the gods and goddesses pictured in the magazines. They are permanently smooth, slim and beautiful, and even when they have children appear to remain so. There are two reasons for this. One, they exercise all the time and never relax. And Two, they never eat. Oh, and three: they have picture control.

If you think I'm exaggerating, I read an interview with Liza Minnelli a couple of years ago in which she described her lunch as 'water and a piece of fruit'. And this was while tap dancing for ten hours a day. That was bad enough, except she had the same for breakfast and dinner as well. Well, that sure is how to put the 'hearse' in 'rehearse'. It's no wonder people stand around going, *'Isn't she amazing?'* because she is. She's alive. I tried that diet. I was in a hypoglycaemic coma by teatime. Remember the Duchess of Windsor, who said, *'You can never be too rich or too thin'*? Well, she was wrong because you can. You can be dead.

As someone who has willpower *issues* – as in no willpower – I know full well that you aren't a Grown-up if you don't curb your appetites. Appetites have to be kept under control, like pets. And I just find that too hard. I managed to get very drunk on dessert wine one New Year's Eve, and I don't even like it, although in fairness it was a particularly good one. It's just a pity it comes in those tiny little bottles, so no one else was able to have any. And it isn't just cake, chocolate and wine; it's anything I happen to take a fancy to at a given moment. Years ago, I smoked so much dope I fell down the stairs at a nightclub, and was only saved from worse misfortune by a kindly bouncer who took me outside and held my hand while I was sick. (Leroy, if you're reading this: thanks for not minding about the shoes.) And I once ate about three pounds of strawberries at a Pick Your Own farm. I didn't throw up, but I did walk to the car very slowly, and – you may be horrified to hear this – ate about another pound that evening with cream. Also, when I was young and we never had white bread at home, whenever I could get it I'd consume huge amounts. My friend Claudia, whose mother always had particularly nice bread, used to watch in somewhat stunned silence as I would polish off an entire loaf, slice by slice.

I still keep hoping I'll grow out of it. Last year I was taken for a Very Grown-up lunch, with some Americans who think nothing of flying for eight hours just to eat oriental food. Well, to eat oriental food while Taking a Meeting. The restaurant was *very* Grown-up. I was turned away from it once when I was in town with a friend when we were looking for somewhere to have a drink. It had been written up in *Time Out* as a cool bar with high-concept nibbles or something, but they wouldn't let us in. This time they did, though.

It was all lined with dark wood, without quite

enough light, a bit like being in a very large cupboard. Staff-wise, it followed the precept of the old Eastern Bloc: a job for everyone as long as they wear the same jacket. They had a person to look up your reservation in the book, a person to take your coat, a person to put *away* your coat and a person who did nothing but open the door to the loos. In there, it was *so* dark you had to feel your way up the door to find the lock. Instead of sinks they had one long ceramic trough, with branches of some kind of tree strewn around. The dimness was definitely flattering, I'll give them that, though I did hurt my neck twisting round to get my mouth into a tiny patch of light so I could do my lipstick.

I came out and coolly ordered a main course costing £34, as if I do it every day, while my hosts summoned the dim sum special for starters. When these arrived – juicy, delicious little dumplings full of yumminess – I completely forgot what I was doing and ate *loads*. I wasn't quite Homer Simpson, but you know that moment when the rest of the room just goes into a blur? Actually, now I think about it, I always eat like that. The first time Peter and I ever spent the night together, I found these After Eights by the bed and went into a bit of a trance. He came back in with the coffee to find the box empty, and even then I remember thinking: *I've probably blown the relationship already, but those After Eights were so yummy.* Mmmm! Where was I? Oh yes: I looked up to see the people from LA trying not to stare. Two were politely nibbling, while one did the even more Grown-up thing, which is to order food then have it taken away.

So if you want to be like Liza Minnelli, or any famous thin person, let me leave you with the *Ultimate Serenity Diet*. It could get you to Heaven that bit sooner.

DAY ONE

Breakfast: Mix a teaspoon of oats with some skimmed water.

Lunch: Steam a flake of sea bass.

Dinner: Place a raspberry beside a piece of melon.

DAY TWO

Breakfast: Infuse some leaves of fennel.

Lunch: Place an apple segment next to a slice of cucumber.

Dinner: Arrange a sprig each of fresh basil, celery and spinach.

DAY THREE

Breakfast: Pour some warm water into a glass. Move it away.

Lunch: Pick a flower. Contemplate the petals.

Dinner: Gaze up at the sky. Look down again. Breathe.

Repeat for the next ten days, making sure not to alternate lunch with dinner, and vice versa. Die.

18 The Scream

They say the human animal takes so long to mature because it has such a large brain, which'll be news to anyone who's ever tried to get after-sales service at Curry's. Well, all right: if that's the case, then why doesn't it work? During all those supposedly developmental years, what is the human offspring actually *doing*? In my case, snogging. Instead of maturing, I was lying on sofas kissing boys; months at a time, clamped to someone else's gob. It seems incredible now. And when I wasn't doing that, I was with my friend Tilly over at her house, drinking Bacardi and Coke, eating chocolate crispy cake and arguing over who was better, Stevie Wonder or The Soft Machine.

Now, I may not be a Normal Female, but that doesn't mean I don't have feelings. Yet I'm having to contend with daily assaults on my self-image by the children, who fail to understand that a forty-year-old woman is *sensitive*.

'I like your tummy,' for example, says Lawrence.

'Oh, do you darling? That's nice.'

'Yes. I like wobbly, squashy things.'

And on another day:

'I hate to tell you this, Mummy. But you really do look better with your clothes *on*.'

Note the 'I hate to tell you this'. The next thing I know, he'll be leaning over his cappuccino saying, *'I'm only telling you this as a friend.'*

And let's not leave out Lydia's contribution:

'Your roots are going grey again even though you've just done them, Mummy. It must be because you're getting quite old.'

I can't complain. A woman in a charity shop has just told me her granddaughter asked her what it was like when the Romans were here. No, I can. And I will.

Of course, because of this unusual time we live in where parents and children listen to the same music, read quite a few of the same books and watch the same films, I've been able to delude myself that I'm really not that much older than them. The new series of *Dr Who* is on, and we all stop fighting to watch the trails.

'That lady kissed Dr Who!' exclaims Lydia during the latest one.

'There was no kissing in my day,' I say, and Lawrence retorts:

'That's because Dr Who was – like, *sixty*.'

I had a touch of flu in the winter, and discovered there's nothing like lying prone on the bed in extreme discomfort to make you appreciate your former vigour. The children gathered round, Lydia leaning forward to voice her concern at this rare sign of maternal infirmity:

'Mummy, when you die,' she said, 'can I have your diamond-y earrings?'

My appetite had been off for a couple of days, so I was worried I might be in danger of getting that scary side-effect of the ageing process which my sister calls the Sunken Look, where people start out like Victoria Beckham and end up like Edvard Munch's *The Scream*. But no: by the end of day two I was wolfing down beer and chicken tikka, having therefore also missed what was probably my final chance to deploy her strategy for Ageing Well.

'You have to start thin and fill out,' she explained, 'like Catherine Deneuve.' And indeed, Catherine Deneuve looks great. But then, *she's Catherine Deneuve*. And anyhow, I blew the 'start thin' part of it thirty years ago.

So I say *this*. If I'm going to have to contend with constant reminders of my physical deterioration, while not being granted the emotional maturity even to deal with a simple visit to the doctor, I want some kind of compensation.

I've seen what hitting forty can do to men of previously good character – the preposterous cars, the seedy affairs. So I'm taking steps to customize my Midlife Crisis in a way that's compatible with the schedule of a modern, working mother. Since I don't want an affair or a smaller, faster car, I've decided that flirting is the way forward. That way, I can get through my forties not as a sad divorcee with a car that's too small for her, but as a still-married, not entirely pathetic specimen with some belief in her own sex appeal. Well, a *bit*. I just have to remember not to look to the children for any reassurance about my appearance.

As a coping mechanism flirting has a lot going for it. I get some male attention, and Peter gets a reminder that other men do occasionally notice me, so he should keep the compliments coming in case I ever start to feel *unappreciated*. I like to keep the merest hint of an exit strategy just lurking in the background. It's a bit like the argument Thatcher made for Trident; you may not like it, you may not wish to use it, but aren't you bloody glad it's There? (Actually, no, Margaret, we weren't.)

Anyhow, I've identified two target groups: men I

don't know and probably won't see again – or I hope I don't – and male friends who are in the same boat. That's to say, they don't hate their lives or their wives, but won't say no to being fancied as long as *nothing actually happens*. Equally, they can be single. Mildly suggestive texting is In; turning up at their house when their wife and kids are away in nothing but a basque – corset not separatist – is Out.

There are two reasons I don't want an affair. One, I'm terrible at lying, and infidelity seems to involve a great deal of it. I lied so badly at school I was always whisked off to Detention before I'd got to the end of the sentence. I'm not carefree enough; when I was fifteen, a handsome Frenchman tried to seduce me on a beach in Tunisia, but even at that age I couldn't bear the incursion of all that sand. I'm not cut out for hurried rendezvous in cars – not with my back. And then I get overwhelmed by logistics. I can't organize play dates for my children; how could I possibly manage an affair? Peter and I watched a steamy scene of hotel adultery on TV recently, where the woman rang the man and said, 'I'm in Room 23!' and he drove over there like the clappers. But being in a state he didn't park very carefully. And all I could think was, *He's been in there ages; he'll have got a ticket*. And even if I did get that far, I'd lose my nerve because of guilt – and having to let him see my wobbly tummy. But I'd probably feel I'd *have* to go through with it once the room had been paid for, as if it were a piano lesson.

I'm not even mentioning the teensy-*weensy* consider-ation that no one's actually asked me.

Still, I'm trying to cultivate a trousers half-full kind of outlook. I got hooked on flirting as a kind of methadone to the heroin of actual infidelity when I was mistaken for thirty-three at a wedding, admittedly during a power cut. I was thirty-nine at the time. I thought: *I've found the Secret of Eternal Youth! No Lights!* The next time we had a party, I turned them down so far we had to feel our way to the food. And while I obviously *never* do that teenage thing of organizing an entire event to meet one person, I'll admit I had half an eye on the attractive actor who had just moved in opposite. I slipped an invitation under his door, including his wife's name – in very small letters – and envisaged myself laughing adorably while he regaled me with hilarious filming stories, despite our whole relationship hitherto having consisted of his smiling at me while putting out his recycling.

'Go easy on him,' was Peter's parting shot, as I

sailed down the stairs in a cloud of Dior that would fell a train of commuters faster than anthrax.

He didn't come, of course. When I did see him several days later, I was unloading a second-hand plastic castle from the car and shouting at the children. Also, as Lydia pointed out afterwards, you could see my tummy bulging over my jeans.

Still, the party went well. I definitely did 'score' a few times, that is until a friend of mine *who shall remain nameless* turned up in a miniskirt and with five fewer years on the clock, at which point quite a lot of the men began to move in slow motion. Even so, I refused to let my optimism be dented. I was continuing to nurture the illusion that I could pull off that trick of the light anywhere. It's like film stars having picture control; they only release shots of themselves looking fabulous, so can delude themselves that they do still really look that good.

The only problem with this strategy, of course, is (a) when you start to believe it, and (b) when you have to go into daylight. If you're not careful you stop looking in mirrors and end up wafting about staring wide-eyedly like Norma Desmond in *Sunset Boulevard*, with only a loyal retainer for company, who's equally mad. On the other hand, if the loyal retainer is Erich von Stroheim, maybe that's not such a bad deal. I'd stay indoors for a few years with him.

Just to avoid any confusion, I don't actually want to Be Young Again. I don't miss that kind of excitement. When I was sixteen, eighteen, around there, going out was an endurance test of how long you could stay up, dancing and kissing – and fiddling – before having to be dragged out and folded into a night bus at 5 a.m., with your tights being posted on to you later. I don't miss that, and I don't have unreasonable expectations. Honestly. All I want is to have a forty-year-old mind inside a thirty-year-old body. Or the forty-year-old mind I would have, if I weren't so immature.

19 But I'm Not *Old* Enough
for a Midlife Crisis

From time to time, Peter ventures into the closet opposite the attic and, wistfully stroking the red silk edged with black velvet, says: 'Your wedding dress really is lovely. Why don't you ever wear it any more?'

'Well, let me see. Oh, yes: IT'S THREE SIZES TOO SMALL. Does that clear up the mystery at all?'

It's an endearing characteristic of men that they have no idea what size you are. It's annoying, I'll grant you, if they come back from a trip to New York with a fabulous set of underwear that doesn't fit and can't be changed. But for a marriage, it can only be a Good Thing. Because for the woman of, as the French put it, *Un Certain Age*, trying to come to terms with what's happening to her body is nothing short of traumatic. And that's without the added insult of the British sizing system.

I'm bigger round the bust than the bum, so the jackets of suits never fit, the cheap ones especially, because they're cut so skimpily. Plus my tummy has its own size – Extra Large – and its own centre of gravity, which, with the advancing years, is not anywhere nearer my face. Meanwhile my arms, which I never used to have to think about, are billowing outwards. Remember 'combination skin'? I've got a Combination Body. Most of us have.

But the fashion industry's not interested. So buying clothes is somewhat of a challenge. Add to that the forty-something's ordeal of trying to find stuff that's neither Britney nor Widdecombe, but something in between, and you get *stressed*.

Browsing the rails in Hobbs one day, I hear one of the sales assistants tell a customer, 'Size 16 is the biggest we do, though obviously we don't have everything in that size.'

No, why would you? It's only the national average. So incredibly *big* of you even to let us in the door!

What's particularly galling about this is that men, who *want* to be Large, or at least not Small, have perfectly sane sizing, while women – who mostly think they're huge even when they're not – have this absurd system that basically ends in the middle. Yes, there are chains, Marks & Spencer notably, that do 18–22 as a matter of routine. But the shops with a touch more chic? No way.

No wonder every woman I meet is on a bloody diet; she can't squeeze into these stupidly labelled clothes. Imagine, for a moment, that the sizes were simply shuffled along a bit. How would you feel about that size 16 now, if it was labelled a 12? A damn sight better, right? So why can't our system be altered to the American model? Over there, I'm a 10. I'd move there immediately, only I don't like the politics, education system, healthcare costs, religious fundamentalism, coffee or hair. But we could do it here; it's such an easy little thing too. Imagine: it's possible to raise the self-esteem of half the population, but oh no, it would involve *changing the labels*. Oh well, never mind, eh.

Still, you have to wear something. And besides, if you're planning a Midlife Crisis you ought to dress for it. I decided to start with a new bra, anecdotal research – peering at people from behind my paper – having revealed that there's nothing more ageing than low-flying breasts. Shove them up a level and you take ten years off, easy. Or at least five. OK, three: that's my final offer. Actually, why stop there? Reverse the Ageing Process! Hang upside down like a bat. In the size that my bosoms have settled down to, post breastfeeding and post various feeble attempts to lose the tummy –

i.e. giving up chips for two days – I am exactly in between a 34C and a 36B: a 35B and a half. In a 34C, the flesh just behind my armpits hangs unattractively over the sides, but the breasts stay up just right. In a 36B there are no overhangs, but the bust is a peg lower, like a shelf unit put together in the dark.

So I got a 34C and practised pulling my back in more, though not as far as, say, Barbara Windsor. I had a slipped disc twenty years ago, and know that even *more* ageing than saggy bosoms is limping around dosed to the eyeballs with codeine, followed by whimpering and collapsing on the floor.

And flush with success at having achieved the bra, I recklessly went back to Hobbs, where I tried on a pink striped, stretchy, cardigan-style top. This I reckoned I could get away with, because (a) the sleeves covered my increasingly substantial upper arms, and (b) the top could be unbuttoned to Draw the Eye Down away from my short neck and towards the not entirely horrible bust. I experimented with the buttons, and found two useful settings: two undone, for school run and general use, and three undone, for evenings and taking out the rubbish at the same time as the man who lives opposite.

At the cash desk the young and abnormally tall Scandinavian sales assistant tried to interest me in the matching camisole, which I'd already passed on due to not wanting to look *too* stripey, i.e. like a tube of toothpaste, some of which has squirted out.

'No thanks,' I said. 'When you get to my age, well, you know what works and what doesn't.' She fiddled slightly uncomfortably with that pointless tissue they wrap things in which doesn't stop them ending up in a crushed heap at the bottom of the bag.

'You're not – old,' she ventured, a little too uncertainly.

He-*llo*?

'I *know*,' I said tersely. 'I'm just saying that at my age you know what works.'

'Exercise?' she began.

'Look, I walk half an hour to school every day, and half an hour back actually. I'm not in need of – advice. And I meant *clothes*.'

'Oh, right. Well, that's great.'

She scrunched the rest of the tissue into the carrier and shoved it across the counter.

I walked away, plunged into gloom. She was abnormally *tall*, I told myself; she wasn't even pretty!

Should I look at some trees? That might cheer me up. I decided to walk through Cavendish Square, but faltered when I realized it was full of builders. Almost every inch of grass was covered by men in yellow hats eating sandwiches and, rather daintily, swigging water out of little bottles. In the past I would have freaked – tried to turn back or go the long way round. As a teenager I was not only a bit overweight but horrendously aware of my bosoms which were larger than all my friends'. Should I hide? No need! In my magic, Forty-Year-Old Cloak of Invisibility I passed completely unscathed.

Beware of What You Wish For: You May Get It. This is what you always wanted, I told myself. When I was sixteen, and men leaned out of lorries to shout, '*You don't get many of them to the pound!*' I'd have given anything to be ignored. Hang on: maybe builders just have got politer. After all, don't they have those signs on some sites these days, saying something like, '*Westminster Considerate Builders Scheme: We Promise Not to Shout at Your Tits*'?

Yeah, right. You're forty: *GET USED TO IT*. When you run, your *face* moves. I went through a brief period of speculating whether, if I ever had the money, I'd have it lifted. But then I saw a picture of a female MP in the newspaper. The story was about MP's expenses, but all I could think was: '*I'm sure her eyes didn't used to be different heights.*'

Feeling quite pert and perky in my new bra, with pink top in bag, I arrive at John Lewis to buy a phone. The buttons on the old one have got more and more sluggish, until to dial an eight-digit local number is taking up to twenty increasingly impatient stabs at the keypad, followed by Peter throwing it down the stairs.

'See? I told you we need a new phone.'

My expectations of domestic communications technology have been severely lowered now; no back-handed compliments or advice on fitness, thanks very much: just a phone. I am served by a chirpy young man who listens to my requirements and shows me several. They are either white and clunky, like the one at the bottom of our stairs, or silver and tiny, like Captain Kirk's communicator, but even smaller and more science-fictional. I can't read any of the displays.

There's nothing else for it.

'The thing is,' I say, 'they're all too complicated. When you get to my age you just want a *phone*. You don't want to do six manoeuvres just to set the outgoing message.' He looks at me, confused. Have I now had a stroke and am talking rubbish?

'Er, how d'you mean, "your age"?' he says, finally. 'Aren't you about the same age as me?'

Is this for real? Have the other assistants put him up to it as a dare? I glance round the side of the counter for signs of convulsed salespersons, egging him on. What have I got to lose?

'And – gulp – what age is *that*?'

'Thirty-one.'

Well, you can imagine. I nearly kiss him. Luckily I hold back but can't resist a small, unchoreographed skip, of the kind not generally seen outside old Eurovision Song Contest routines.

'Oh my God! That's so fantastic! *Thank you!*' I go on like this until the supervisor looks over, possibly in shock at someone finding a phone they could actually work out how to use.

'That's quite all right, madam,' he says, edging away. He takes the *BT Autologic with 100-number memory, SMS facility and granite fascia* to the till for me, and disappears. I float back on a high and tell Peter of my triumph.

'That's nice,' he says. 'Did you get the phone?'

Clearly, I need more. Flirting is addictive, and I am hooked. And I get my chance soon afterwards, on my way to meet Peter and some friends for a drink. He's told me the bar is 'round the corner' from Victoria Station, which it isn't. It's a long walk, and I'm in heels. I see a bus and run after it – without actual lung pain, though definitely breathing like someone who hasn't run anywhere since 1979. I explain to the driver that I don't have a pass and need to go to the top of the road. I fish out the fare but he waves it away.

'*Just stay by me,*' he says, and winks.

He looks young enough – just about – to be my son. He is also scrawny and bullet-headed, like Ross Kemp crossed with a whippet. But that does nothing to dim my inner glow. As we hurtle along, I lean against the bulletproof glass like a getaway driver's moll, trying not to be swung onto the floor like a bad impression of Norman Wisdom.

I'll swear he drives away reluctantly. Or possibly having driven too fast, he is now ahead of schedule and has to slow down. Still, when I get to the bar, I am brought down to earth by another sign of physical degeneration: my inability, in a noisy room, to hear. Put me in a full restaurant with wooden floors and I pretty much have to lip-read.

The nice-looking barman asks what I want, with what seems an Inviting Look.

'Where are you from?'

'Albania.'

'Albania! Mmm!'

Almost Erich von Stroheim territory, but without the monocle and leather boots. By now I am in full Norma Desmond Mode, but it doesn't seem to matter.

I go and show my age anyhow, by asking him to turn down the music, or change it to something that doesn't sound like furniture being pushed down the stairs.

I can't see Peter, and not wanting to bring the fun to an end, I give the barman one of my cards for the Bad Mothers Club. He calls over his mate, who takes one look at the woman with the glass and dummy, and positively drools. They look at each other.

'When does it open?!'

Lovely idea, though I do obviously explain that it's an online support network, not a menopausal bordello patrolled by sexually voracious women in comfortable shoes. Maybe that was the bus driver's thing, too. He didn't think I looked young at all, but was in the grip of some kind of Mrs Robinson Syndrome. Still, if I can get Peter to notice it will all have been worthwhile. Eventually I stroll over with my drink.

'Where've you been?'

'Oh, just – at the bar. The barman's Albanian.'

'Oh? If you were having trouble getting served, you should have come and got me.'

'Oh, never mind.'

I told him about the bus driver.

'He *definitely* fancied me.'

'Oh, well done!' he says, as if about to give me a 'Good Effort' sticker. The Midlife Crisis is under way.

20 Time Is a Bloody Shifty Bastard

The film *Big* comes into my mind quite a lot. There's a
scene in the middle of it where Elizabeth Perkins, who's
fallen in love with Josh, the Tom Hanks character, is
trying to explain to his uptight rival why she's so keen
on him. Getting more and more frustrated with his
failure to appreciate the new guy, she says in exaspera-
tion, 'He's a *Grown-up*.'

And of course the audience laughs because *we* know
that Josh is in fact a thirteen-year-old boy.

When I was about to be thirteen, I made a list of
things I wanted for my birthday, which I gave to my
dad. It had on it, among other things, a Winnie the
Pooh calendar and a training bra, and he thought this
very telling about the transitional nature of puberty,
blah blah blah. What he couldn't have known, of course,
was that I would stay at that stage.

At the age of nine, I was best friends with a girl
called Thalia and we were – some years before *Charlie's*

Angels – Model-Detectives. We zoomed around in jet-propelled, gold sports cars and had cosmetics that turned into weapons. That was really the high point, being the Most Beautiful Women in the World and able to catch baddies. It was never the same after that.

When I was a child, I couldn't wait to grow up because I thought how great it'd be, being able to stay up as late as I liked, every night, and having the money to buy as many sweets as I wanted. I often ponder the irony of this when I'm in a shop not buying chocolate because it's bad for me, or nodding off in front of the TV because I can't stay awake beyond half past nine. It invites the rather unsettling possibility that you don't always want what you thought you did. Dreams *can* come true. They just aren't always dreams any more when they do.

When I was fourteen, I briefly fulfilled my desire to become an actor, and discovered it was rather harder than it looked. I thought being in a play would be glamorous and exciting. In fact, I said my few lines very badly, I couldn't walk properly because my shoes were too big and had been stuffed with newspaper, and while I was doing my scene someone got into the dressing rooms and stole my bus money. And this was BBC2.

A couple of years later, I had similarly high hopes of losing my virginity. My boyfriend at the time was in his twenties, with an MGB and the sort of flat you see now in post-ironic-retro magazine spreads: white carpets, smoked glass table and a round telly on a stalk. It took me a good few months to realize he was a twat. He was even quite good-looking, but this was counteracted by a delusion that he resembled Paul McCartney. And bear in mind this was at the time of Wings. He claimed that people stared at him because of it, whereas if they were staring at him, which was doubtful, it was because they were thinking, *What a twat*. Thank God he chucked me in the end and I was able to move on.

One fantasy that has survived intact is my love for Marc Bolan. When I was twelve, my deepest wish in life was to marry him, to which end I bought a T-shirt with his picture on it and stood outside his office with a friend on the grounds that it doubled our chances. Whichever one of us he chose, the other would at least be able to ride in the Rolls. Our relationship was never sullied by any actual contact, and when I saw him by chance on a *Top of the Pops* retrospective, it was as if the thirty intervening years had been sucked into the box.

I think, just as computers have internal modems, I have an internal Tardis which shoots me around in time.

'Mummy, are you old?' Lydia asks.

'Well! A bit I suppose. It all depends how you—'

'Have you already *been* young?'

The children see everything in terms of stages. Their lives are defined by them. It's not just the obvious things like learning to use the loo, or starting school or getting their own ice creams out of the freezer. Growing up is entirely about graduating to the next stage, and very thrilling it is too. The year before last, Lawrence stood in the playground and said, 'I can't believe I'm in 3A!'

And Lydia said wistfully, the night before she became five: 'I'll never be four again . . .'

And when she was nearly four, she said, 'I don't want to be a Little Girl.'

And I said, 'You can have lots of fun as a Little Girl! Then you'll be a Big Girl, then a Grown-up Lady.'

'And then I'll shout, *"Don't bounce on the bed"* like you!'

It's all about having something to look forward to. Then last year:

'Can I have a tankini?'

'Not now, no. Maybe when you're older.' *Yeah, right.* 'You've got to have something to look forward to.'

'You've got to spread it out in your life!'

'That's it!'

'You can't have it all bunched up in your Childish Life.'

They have such an intense sense of forward momentum that even things which to anyone else would be arbitrary – *are* abitrary – are fixed firmly in their minds in a precise sequence. For example, not too long ago, when she was in Year 2, I said to Lydia: 'Did you know that after Charles I had his head cut off, Oliver Cromwell was the Ruler, and he closed the theatres and wouldn't let anyone have any fun?'

'What?!' she snapped. 'Why are you telling me THAT??!'

'Because it's about the Stuarts. Your Topic.'

'We're not doing the Stuarts any more!'

'Oh. Sorry. What are you doing, then?'

'MAGNETS!'

As far as she's concerned, they go *in that order*. Hence she is able to experience the reassuring sensation of constantly moving forward. I, however, am not. I am going backwards, sideways – all over the place. She also associates getting older with growing, which is why she asked the other day why I don't regularly add my height to the tally we keep by the bathroom door.

'There's no point,' I explained. 'I stopped growing thirty years ago.'

'Stopped *growing*??!'

She can't imagine it. Well, come to think of it, neither can I. I was under the impression that I would go on becoming more mature. I certainly thought forty would be more Grown-up than thirty. A 'Matured Funds Statement' for the children's savings accounts recently came through the door, and I thought how great it would be if I could have one saying: *Stephanie Calman has now Matured*, with a nice official stamp. I could carry it around, and it could comfort me in all those situations which bring out the child in me – which, thinking about it, is nearly all of them.

For once, Peter has some sympathy. He was pulled over on his way back from a party a while back for doing 34 mph in a dinner jacket.

'I instantly became eighteen again,' he recalled, 'but not in a good way. Like some sheepish new driver, nervous of the policeman – who was, of course, much younger than me.'

As I say, the children experience almost constant forward momentum. And so do we, but tragically only physically.

One morning I slipped getting into the shower, and aged about thirty years in one go. One minute I was skipping along in my slinky nightie, feeling – you know, *OK*. Then I put one foot in, the so-called anti-slip thing slid away from me – and I sort of did the splits, slamming a leg painfully against the edge of the bath. I felt like Ursula Andress – Ursula Andress at the end of *She*, that is, where she goes into the Eternal Flame twice – which she's been warned *not to do*, and in about thirty seconds turns from voluptuous blonde sex siren into shrivelled old hag, and from that into skeleton and, finally, dust. It was a sobering moment. Still, I suppose if you're going to have a life flash before you, hers isn't a bad one to have.

As Peter rescued me the children looked on, shaking their heads.

'Have you broken anything?' he said.

'I think I'm just very bruised.'

'Welcome to my World,' Lawrence sighed. He'd just turned eight.

I'd like to have said that going around with a purple knee made me feel just like an eight-year-old boy – in a Good Way. But I'd be lying. Even after Lawrence collided with the radiator, meaning we walked to school with matching limps, we couldn't have been mistaken for peers. He limped cheerfully, checking his bruise every few yards to make sure it hadn't faded before we reached the playground, while I trudged mournfully, a cartoon sign above my head saying, *'Decrepitude: This Way'*. I thought of something my sister said once.

'I had spots,' she reflected, 'which after adolescence

never went away. And now I've got lines round my eyes. So I've got spots *and* lines. What happened to the period of clear skin in between?'

And here I am with my bruised knee, feeling like an old woman, while my personality hasn't matured at all. It doesn't seem fair. And to *really* put the lid on it, that was my good knee.

If only we were caterpillars. We'd go to bed all spotty and hormonal, spend six months wrapped in a duvet – and emerge in a suit. It's a great system. One day you're crawling along a lettuce, the next you're soaring over the countryside. Caterpillar: butterfly. There's no confusion. It's digital. The human condition is horribly analogue.

I've said children develop in strictly defined, incremental stages – but not all. Some are old beyond their years. Children with old men's faces. Small boys in Morocco who can smoke, sell oranges and molest you all at the same time. Peter had a friend who when he was ten, taught himself to drive. In adolescence, some of us rush too fast onto the next stage. We can't wait to drink, smoke and get laid. I was dead keen to do those things, which was stupid because not one of them lived up to expectations. But I think, *Hang on, I should be allowed some of that time back*. Then, I speeded up. Now, I'm ready to slow down. It's like the university grant I didn't take up. I should be able to have it now, put it towards a new car or something. But, oh no. You can go back all right – just never in the way you want. Because Time is a Bloody Shifty Bastard. Think of the least honourable person you ever slept with, the one who dumped you the next day and wouldn't even look you in the eye. It's worse.

You know it is, because: that moment when the alarm goes off and you shut your eyes *just for a second*? Then, when you wake up again, you've missed the train and lost your job? It's because Time is not Constant. The physicists tell us it can be Bent. Well, you said it, mate. And if any of them have ever done the school run, they'll know that Time gets longer and shorter, like a confused willy, depending on your age.

If you are a woman without children who wants them, you will notice that each year of your thirties, however much you achieve, is shorter than the year before. If conception occurs, the process is temporarily reversed. The moment an egg is fertilized, Time slows down and nine months seem like nine years. But carry on without, and it eventually goes so fast that the menopause is here before you can say, '*I haven't had a period for eight months: could I have left it a teensy bit late?*'

Assuming a pregnancy does take place, the labour may well involve distorted Mutant Minutes that last five times as long as any pain you've ever known. Toothache, being run over, falling down a lift shaft – all pass in the twinkling of an eye in comparison with the time it takes a baby to pass through an opening designed to take nothing wider than a Tampax. And afterwards? The nights pass quickly or slowly, depending on baby's propensity to sleep. Breast- and bottle-feeding minutes are of course not the same, and Colic Minutes are in fact Hours, literally sixty times as long, while for a baby the gaps between feeds are not minutes or hours, but Days.

Then, for a child aged between one and four, the length of Time between your saying, *'Would you like a biscuit?'* and actually finding it and giving it to them is Very, Very Long, whereas the Time they spend lying on the floor screaming when it doesn't arrive flashes by in the blink of an eye. But the Time spent *watching* a toddler having a tantrum is Very Long if you're their parent, Extremely Long if you're not their parent, and Infinite if you have no children at all. Children who continue to have prolonged tantrums beyond the age of three, or who do not grow out of biting, or do not learn to share, have become stuck in Toddler Time. They are happy to while away half an hour or more on the floor yelling, whereas an older child will generally get bored and find something more interesting to do. If they're still doing it as adults, they're best avoided and on no account should be given countries to run.

Gender is also a factor. People who appear to inhabit the same Time–Space Continuum can be on different planes altogether. This is why men generally perceive silences in conversation as Quite Short, while women experience them as great, gaping chasms. It's part of the reason why women make long phone calls to the person they're going to have lunch with in two hours, and men can get through entire Christmases without uttering a word.

Not convinced? Take the two or so hours between getting up in the morning and arriving at the school gate. They *seem* long enough, but aren't. This is because they're made up of Short Minutes, which are basically Seconds. But you're stuck with them; no matter how much you hurry, no matter how many packed lunches/ PE kits/Viking longships you put together the previous night, there is never enough time. It's an empirical fact.

The time when you've dropped children off is supposedly quite generous; five hours – four if you discount getting back – sounds like loads. And indeed, if you're having a smear test or doing your tax return, they are. But go to a nice tidy office or lunch with an ex-boyfriend and *whoosh*! Suddenly it's three thirty and you're pounding up the pavement to collect a sobbing, red-faced kid whose whole sense of security has been destroyed. Or once, in my case, zooming through the door and grabbing my own child, leaving behind the poor, snivelling mate who'd been invited to tea. Whereupon Time contracted *again*, leaving no minutes at all before the kid's mother was on the phone telling me what she thought of *that*.

Spool forward to 4 p.m.-ish, and the Long March towards children's bedtime. Four crawls towards five ... Five eventually becomes six ... These are Long Minutes, so-called because you can actually see the clock slowing down. It's the opposite of warp speed; the stars and planets don't go into white lines and whoosh past the camera, but stay so still you can see the Clangers watering their plants. By seven, you're beginning to think your children will be up for the rest of their lives. Teeth brushing, finding and putting on pyjamas, excavating a roomful of toys for that one cuddly zebra without which sleep is an impossibility – all take ten times as long as any sane person has a right to expect. You rush through a story, defying all known laws not just of Time, but narrative structure – '*Isn't there a Prince in* Cinderella, *Mummy?*' – and emerge gratefully into the evening.

Then, at the precise moment you shut the door on

them, Time is up to its old tricks again! At around eight o'clock, or whenever it is that you reach the wine box, it has already begun to speed up. Telly? Newspapers? Sex, or even a nice, juicy book? You'd better get moving because Time is most emphatically not on your side. There *is* one way of slowing down Time in the evenings. You can switch on the iron. Or you could just argue with your kids until they – and you – crash out.

'I am old,' I concede, 'but I'm a Time Lord. So I get older then younger again.'

'You're not a Time Lord,' says Lawrence. 'You're embarrassing.'

'OK, well can you please pick up your clothes and put them in the dirty washing box?'

'Do I have to do *everything* round here?'

The boy is eight going on forty, I'm telling you. But then, aren't we all?

21 The £55 Trainers

I often think about what Billy's father said in the park that day, about Not Arguing. His words have really stayed with me. What a shame they've had no effect.

I have always said – we both have – that we will never buy the children expensive or designer clothes, and especially not get caught up in the mania for very costly, and ultimately pointless, trainers. We would never, for example, spend £55 on one pair. Earlier this year, however, we did.

It was Peter's fault.

Lydia started coming into our room and complaining that she couldn't sleep in their room any more, because the milk float made a scary noise. She said its strange whiney sound was waking her up. She and Lawrence were sharing the big bedroom at the front, as they always had, while we had the admittedly quieter room at the back. And she was gathering up her soft toys at 4 a.m. or whenever, and taking up residence in there. She was also doing it on the nights the milkman didn't deliver.

'But Lydia, you don't wake up *every* time.'

'Yes, I do!'

'No, you don't. He doesn't even come on Wednesday or Friday, so how can you?

'He DOES!'

'He doesn't. So maybe it isn't that, maybe it's just a bad dream.'

'It isn't a bad dream! He does come, he *DOES*!'

The knock-on effect of this was that Lawrence was waking up, complaining that he couldn't sleep because he was on his own. This is the point where people say we should have put them in separate rooms from the start, but I'm sorry; I grew up sharing a room, and it was good enough for me. Well, OK, not exactly; my sister and I used to fight viciously and throw things at each other over the bookcase. But anyhow, separate rooms for small children just always seemed to me unnecessary. And I liked having a spare room; it had pretty floral curtains and was a lovely place to just sit in and stare at the garden – if you trod carefully so as not to trip over the bits of shelving that fell off the wall when we moved in, and turned your head slightly so you couldn't see the Sky dish.

Lydia refused absolutely to sleep at the front any more, and moved into the spare room. So we agreed to let it be her room. One of them was going to have to move out eventually, and it did have flowery curtains, so that was OK. But Lawrence wasn't happy. He was now alone in a big room, and while Lydia's was pink and cosy, his was large and echoey. So we offered to refurbish it.

The room had never been decorated, and was still our predecessors' splotchy yellow – remember stippling? We figured if he chose a new colour and maybe a rug to co-ordinate, he'd embrace the room, feel at one with it and go to sleep. He chose blue, a rather strong blue, but that was fine. Peter was going to paint it, but he was busy, so we paid someone else to do it. And he and Lawrence chose a co-ordinating rug, although it was not so much co-ordinating as multicoloured, with big, clashing coloured squares. But he wanted it, so fair enough.

And just after they bought it, he confided that the real reason he couldn't sleep in there wasn't really the colour, it was the bed. It was too high. He and Lydia both had cabin beds which Peter had bought on impulse in an Ikea sale. They were too high, though, so he chopped them down a bit and fitted the little matching desks and drawer units underneath. He went to loads of trouble, and they looked really good. And the children liked sleeping in them, although they never sat at the little desks – even when they were given their own light each as well. Now Lawrence didn't like his any more, and Peter agreed that he had a point, although Lydia was OK because the spare room had its double bed in it which was my old one from when I was single but optimistic.

So Peter offered to get Lawrence a new bed, though when Lydia got wind of this, obviously she had to have one too. Which was fair enough. Katarina happened to pop round at about this time, and mentioned that *her* bed, the old spare one from our previous house, was really uncomfortable and falling apart. So we offered her the spare room one, which would work out brilliantly.

So Peter and I went to Ikea, and drank the horrible coffee with free refills, and bought two really exciting beds which the children had chosen out of the catalogue, because they had three sides to turn into a daybed, which made them cosier, *and* storage drawers underneath, *and* an extra bit which pulled out to accommodate a friend. He and I carefully chose a day to go there which was a normal weekday, and so we didn't get overstressed, even when getting the beds off the shelves and queueing to pay, then queueing again for

home delivery. And we went home, and Peter dismantled the high beds – not something everyone can do, as
he reminded me about every ten minutes while he was
doing it – and packed them neatly into the long cardboard boxes from the new ones. And everyone was
happy.

The old beds were offered to the Shaftesbury
Society, who distribute furniture to, among others,
women who have left their husbands on somewhat
stronger grounds than arguing over vegetables, or
reminding people how good they are at DIY.

They were booked to collect them on a Friday,
between one and five, but we had already decided to
get the children from school and go straight to my
mother's, which meant leaving at three. And *why* had
we 'already decided' this? I suggest you ask Peter.
Indeed, I had cancelled a much needed evening with
a female friend to do this, something that a far less
sorted-out person would probably have resented. But,
as I said to Peter on about the third or fourth time we
went over it, 'I don't mind cancelling my evening with
Ursula, so long as we are going straight off to Mum's,
and not waiting for the Shaftesbury Society to collect
the beds.'

'No, no, not at all. I've moved it to between one and
three.'

'You're sure?'

'Mmm. Yes, absolutely.'

'So that's all OK, then?'

'I *told* you, it's all taken care of.'

At 3 p.m. on the Friday, with me flinging clothes into a bag – and not in a *great* mood, as he had done bugger all towards the packing despite not having a job – he says:

'So what are we doing, then?' And *I* say:

'I don't know. Hey! We could always collect the children – seeing as they get OUT IN TWENTY MINUTES.'

'Oh, *sorry*.' (His favourite term of abuse.) 'Only I arranged for the beds to be collected.'

'And I cancelled my night out so we could get onto the M20 and beat the traffic!'

'Well, why doesn't one of us get the children and the other wait in to do the beds?!'

'Or I've got an idea! Why don't we NOT ARRANGE TO HAVE THE BEDS COLLECTED ON THE SAME AFTERNOON WE'RE COLLECT-ING THE CHILDREN AND GOING STRAIGHT TO MY MOTHER'S????'

'Don't worry, I'll never try to help again.'

'No, because I'm going to kill you.'

We leave at 3.15, lips pursed, beds still in the hall,

my evening out with my friend still cancelled – which, as I say, a person who'd had less therapy than I have would resent. Lydia has to be got first. At 3.25, while I'm getting her, Peter, waiting in the car, sees the Shaftesbury Society van drive into our road. It's reminiscent for me of the scene at the end of *American Graffiti*, when Richard Dreyfuss, ambivalently on the plane to college, finally sees his dream girl in the white Thunderbird driving along below. A lifetime of missed opportunities is symbolized by that shot. Nonetheless Peter remains still, his knuckles nestled between his teeth as I drive to Lawrence's school, where I get out and slam the door quite hard. Several people in the playground give me concerned looks, but can be seen quickly making the decision not to say anything.

Half an hour along the South Circular, I realize something.

'Um. I've forgotten to pack Lawrence's trainers.'

'Oh, *great*.'

'Because it's obviously *my* lone responsibility to remember them. It's not as though *you*—'

'Just drop it, will you? Just drop it. Right! We're going back.'

He pulls over abruptly and starts doing a three-point turn. Because of 'MY' forgetfulness, Lawrence either has to spend a muddy weekend in the country in his school shoes, or we all go back. But we *can't* go back. The whole *weekend* is built on not going back. The Shaftesbury Society have already found we're out and gone. And I've cancelled my night out with a friend, which a less serene person ... Wait! I have an idea – the sort of notion mothers have all the time when something is lost, missing, falls off, gets ketchup on it or suddenly breaks.

'We'll stop on the way and buy some!'

A solution! Peter is always saying Time is the most Precious – whatever it is – commodity. The atmosphere thaws. A little way further along, by some miracle, I see a sign for the world's cheapest trainer shop, Shoe Zone, and he pulls over.

'If you see a traffic warden, drive round the block. Oh no! You can't because of the one-way system. You'd better—'

'It'll be fine! Just get the shoes.'

'OK, but if you—'

'JUST GET THE SHOES.'

I hoik Lawrence out of the car, and within about six minutes have acquired a pair of trainers, price: £4.99. I even fly into the bakery next door and get him and his sister a gingerbread man each for Being Good.

And apart from the nagging annoyance that, with two sentient adults in the house, it's my responsibility, and mine only, to pack the shoes, the weekend goes rather well. I don't even have a row with my mother, which ranks it as one of the least emotionally exhausting weekends of the year. Yes, the beds are still uncollected, but the Shaftesbury Society are very nice about it and give us another date. The next few days pass peacefully.

Then a penalty notice arrives for stopping on a Red Route.

'So those trainers didn't cost £4.99 at all.'

'No,' I say, pen gripped tightly as I write a cheque. 'They cost *£54.99.*'

So, it's not that I always have to have the last word or anything, but can I just say we should have done what I suggested in the first place, and cancelled the milk.

22 Go Away Now: Don't Ask Me How

Every time we have a really *bad* row, I briefly envisage life after divorce. Like peering over a cliff and imagining one's body smashed to bits at the bottom, it frightens me so much I promise myself I will never let it get to that stage – although not so much that I stop arguing. This process has also led me to identify what some marriage counsellors call the Trigger Points, as presumably they find it helpful, when trying to stop people splitting up, to use metaphors related to weapons.

Ever since being woken at 4 a.m., early in the relationship, by the sound of running water and groaning when he came into his bathroom to find me clambering into a bath roughly the temperature of the earth's core, Peter has been aware of a time every four weeks when women *suffer*. He was, and remains, hugely sympathetic.

The only part he has a problem with is why everyone else has to suffer too.

Living with me, he soon discovers there are a million negative influences on my mood: no work, too much work, tiredness, loneliness, road rage, pavement rage and feelings-o-failure – like filet-o-fish but less deliciously crunchy.

How the bollocks can he tell when I've got PMT?

After about fifteen years, a solution presents itself. Some friends at work give him a subscription to *Car* magazine, the arrival of whose first issue coincides, he notices, with this nadir in my cycle. So, if not a cure, we at least have an Early Warning System. The moment *Car* plops onto the mat, he takes it and dives for cover.

And having done so, he sets to Thinking.

'Why can't men have periods?' he says at last.

'What, you mean get to be in agony for two days, go up two clothes sizes and generally feel like shit?'

'No! Have a time every month when you can be horrible to everyone and be let off even a smidgeon of responsibility.' He eyes me levelly. 'People have got away with murder.'

'Almost never. And they've generally been women abused for years and years who've finally snapped.'

'I've got Provocation.'

'Being mildly irritated doesn't count.'

'You're not mildly irritating; you're very, very irritating.'

'No, I'm not.'

'Yes, you are.'

'I'm not.'

'Trust me.'

A pause.

'You were the one who threw the chicken pieces.'

'Ah, you can't bring that up.'

'Yeah, and what was the provocation? Oh yes: you were *sick of looking after me*.'

'This isn't fair.'

'Yes, it is.'

After two weeks of nursing me following my exit from hospital after a car accident some years ago, he got compassion fatigue. I think it was the cooking that tipped him. He had to make all my meals, and one day he just couldn't stand it any more. He said (sighing), 'I suppose I'd better get on with Your Lunch.'

And I said: 'Just *my* lunch is it? You don't eat any more?'

And about two minutes later he threw the chicken pieces. The packet broke and there was blood running down the wall – particularly nice when you think we were borrowing someone else's house at the time.

We were on holiday at the start of the trip, and in hospital at the end. Yet it was in many ways one of the least stressful travel experiences we've had.

I hate booking anything, even cinema tickets, because I hate the responsibility, and am constantly seething with resentment against Peter, who leaves all the arrangements to me. Of course, I should follow the advice I always give anyone else in this position: 'Simply don't do it and he'll just have to.'

But if I did, we'd never go anywhere.

And we *would* end up divorced, because I have recently realized, after seventeen years in this relationship, that while you may save money by not going anywhere, you do end up homicidal. It's not that we never have holidays, it's just that we've gone for long periods without any because organizing them is so stressful it pretty much cancels out the effect. They're either expensive, which leaves me spending the whole time worrying about the cost, or labour-intensive, like camping. If I want to sleep badly and take out my own rubbish, I can do it at home. Peter *loves* it, so he's welcome to take the children anytime he likes, while I go somewhere with big, fat beds to fall into and lots of food cooked by other people, preferably chefs.

When you think how many things *can* go wrong, it's a miracle these things work at all. For example, we went to Madeira as a special treat two years ago, and while the kids loved the swimming pool and the *levada* walks, the stay was somewhat blighted for us by the fact that we didn't have connecting rooms but did have automatically slamming doors, so whenever they woke up in the night, which they did, they went into the corridor to reach our room, and were locked out. And I don't know about you, but I think expecting a five- and a six-year-old to have '*Must remember my key card*' uppermost in their mind when they've just had a nightmare and the door shuts behind them at 3 a.m. – is asking a bit much. After three days we moved into one room.

So even when a trip basically goes well there's always something I've overlooked like that, and am left having to worry about. It's ironic, because when the tour operator and I teamed up to make a spectacular mistake over our honeymoon, it was Peter who fixed it.

I booked at the last minute in my usual way. The simple white house with garden in front looked quite charming, so the reality came as somewhat of a shock: a grim, airless box with a feeble shower and no balcony or views, where the choice was between letting in the air and the mosquitoes, or dying of suffocation during the night. There was also no mention of the fact that the owners were not only on site, but operating a market garden. On the first morning we opened the window – to enjoy the optional extra of breathing – to find two men haggling over tomatoes right outside. And I know I am deeply inhibited, but surely most people like *some* privacy during sex? I know there are people who like to pull up in lay-bys to see and be seen by strangers, so I suppose if you were into being asphyxiated *and* being watched, it would have been ideal.

When I failed to pull out of my despair, Peter persuaded the operator to find us something else, and it was way better, thus proving that he is Good at Travel and I am Not. Yet I always do the booking. How appropriate that the system in the workplace by which people are promoted to do jobs they're no good at is known as the Peter Principle.

So last New Year, desperate for some kind of *treat* to alleviate the post-Christmas anticlimax, we splashed out on three nights at one of these upmarket, child-friendly hotels. There are three very good reasons why we've avoided them in the past: one, like most British hotels they're preposterously expensive. Two, they're full of Other People. And three, they might not be perfect. I get so anxious about the outcome, about the possibility of one tiny thing not being right that Peter won't mind but I will, that I get completely wound up.

Plus we're both exhausted and stressed out at the end of the year anyway, and now even more in need of a break because of the strain involved in trying to book it.

I do lots of very detailed research – into facilities, menus, nearby towns for exploring, blah blah, and get quite a long way down the road with a 'superior B&B' which is far cheaper and does 'superb home cooking', but just as I'm about to debit myself down the phone I happen to ask, as an afterthought really, where the accommodation is in relation to the restaurant. We want to be able to linger over that second bottle after the kids are in bed, and I discover it's not even next door. 'It's a very short walk,' says the receptionist, who has clearly never had a bag of peanuts for dinner in her room because her kids were exhausted and hungry at six, while the dining room didn't open till seven. Mind you, she probably isn't married to someone who doesn't care if he misses dinner, either.

The fact that Peter refuses to do *anything* for the arrangements provokes me into a rage. So the week or so leading up to the dates I've booked is punctuated by shouting matches and slammed doors. Other people seem to be able to drive 100 miles to another building without killing each other, but how? I have a feeling it involves not wanting a fabulous treat, then whingeing like a baby when you have to pay for it. But if that *is* the answer, then don't tell me. I'm still hoping some third party will magically appear who takes care of everything. But for now, it's still me, trying to provide the Perfect Adult & Child-Friendly Weekend without grinding my teeth into powder on the way.

Eventually I settle on Blah-di-Blah Manor, a couple of hours' drive from town. The three days it's taken us – me – to book this thing have brought us close to breaking point and we pack extra quickly, as if trying to leave the gloom and anger behind.

I have tried to think of everything. The hotel has a trampoline, swimming pool, table tennis, table football and videos. The room is lovely, though we have to move around it a bit carefully as the two extra beds leave only the narrowest of floor spaces to walk along. Peter is desperate for a nap, so I agree to take Lawrence and Lydia to High Tea, a dubious looking buffet of pasta, fish shapes and bolognese. There was meant to be spaghetti to go with it but by the time we arrive, one minute inside the designated kids' mealtime, it has run out. Ditto the chips that went with the fish shapes. Nevertheless, the children accept their half-meals with surprisingly good grace, and eat very efficiently so they can get to the games room. At 6.30 p.m., just as we pick up the ping-pong bats, a woman in a Blah-di-Blah

Manor T-shirt comes over and tells us the games room is now closed. Lydia accepts this, while Lawrence, lower lip trembling, allows himself to be steered back to the room for a bath. He has a cold coming on, which I'm hoping will slow him down enough to make him easy to put to bed. All the time I am visualizing the dinner with Peter, which even though we're barely speaking to each other, I anticipate as a great treat. He constantly accuses me of being hard to please, but in a way I'm not at all; I don't mind dining with a man I can hardly bear the sight of, as long as there's proper food and drinkable wine – and preferably a tablecloth. In that sense I'm not fussy at all.

But first we have to get there. Our table is reserved for 7.30 since I have managed to remember to do that too, having learned the hard way in seemingly empty country places that on Saturday nights suddenly fill up with fortieth birthdays and huge ruby wedding parties that leave not so much as a crouton at midnight for anyone stupid enough not to book.

But Lawrence and Lydia do not want to be left in the room. They find Nickelodeon and watch that for a bit, but as soon as they see us edging towards the door, rise up like abandoned puppies and beg us to stay. Of the two, Lydia is more susceptible to reason. Tucked up with her menagerie of fur companions she settles, but

Lawrence will have none of it. We don't know why he's so anxious, but even Peter – whose life doesn't revolve around food – is becoming extremely keen for Grown-up Time. Eventually, after a great deal of negotiating and pleading and agreeing to leave on the telly, we get him into bed, and ourselves down to the restaurant.

'After all,' I say, shutting the door firmly, 'this is the whole point of the break.'

Ensconced behind our menus we breathe out slowly, as if careful not to shatter the fragile peace. The food looks good, and we both order duck in olive and Madeira *jus*. Peter hates the word '*jus*' but can overcome his objections long enough to order it. So far we've had fifteen good minutes. And every minute is precious when the effort required to leave our room is like masterminding *The Great Escape*.

We sip our wine. Suddenly, Peter looks pointedly over my shoulder. Lawrence and Lydia, fully dressed, are making their way towards us. Lawrence is weepy, whereas Lydia is chirpy and matter of fact, as if she's another adult just delivering him to us before going back to work. Peter, in Perfect Dad mode, takes them back and gets them undressed and back into bed. Shortly afterwards, Lawrence appears again, fully dressed, this time alone.

'Oh, for God's sake,' says Peter. He takes him back,

and eventually returns. We drink more wine, and nibble the home-made bread. The food can't be long now.

The third time, Lawrence comes in, rushes up to our table, bursts into tears and is sick into the bread basket. We leap up. He does it again. Peter throws a napkin over the epicentre of the splash, and tries to wipe Lawrence's face. Lawrence bats the napkin away and throws up a third time. By now we have the full attention of the other diners, some actually poised with their forks in mid-air as if in a cartoon. I call over the young French waiter. He takes one look at the table and flees.

'I'll deal with it!' says Mr Perfect, and carries Lawrence out, adding over his shoulder: 'You stay there and have a break.'

Oh, *right*. I'll sit here and Have a Break with the newspaper, the rest of the wine, and a flower in a vase – at a table full of sick.

How dare he be so *marvellous*. It makes me look heartless. It's a kind of gift he has. And it's particularly bad, happening in a *restaurant*. It looks to the ignorant bystander as though we knew Lawrence was ill, but were more interested in the duck with olive and Madeira *jus*. And I am *so* heartless I can sit here and read the paper while my child is virtually dying upstairs.

A couple being shown to their table glance at me,

then at the table, and look away. What do they think I am? Presumably a wealthy bulimic who goes into hotels and orders high-priced food to throw up.

I stand up, wrap the whole lot up in the tablecloth and sit back down again. The waiter appears to be hiding in the kitchen until we've gone.

Then I have an idea. I grab the wine and ask the waiter to bring the main course, when it's ready, up to our room. By the time I get up there, Lawrence is in bed chatting away to Peter while Lydia is disappointed at having missed all the excitement.

'Don't worry, Lydia,' he reassures her. 'I'll show you where I was sick tomorrow.'

We have our duck in olive and Madeira *jus* on a tray while watching *Wife Swap* – and it tastes delicious. The room is smart and comfortable – with, obviously, the added advantage over the dining room of not smelling of sick. Now we just have the rest of our treat to get through.

23 Living On the Join

We've been for lunch with an old friend, Alison, and her husband Frank. As Lawrence's first ever babysitter, Alison enabled us to take our first faltering steps to freedom, and therefore has a special significance for us. She also, as a trained hairdresser, gave Lawrence his first haircut, although he does not remember this. As I said at the start, she has done lots of challenging things without whingeing and is therefore a role model for me, though needless to say I am nothing like her.

Frank makes us a delicious lunch, and promises to take Lawrence across the road to the park afterwards to play football. Despite having no children of his own, he is amazingly good with ours. He plays *'Here's the church and here's the steeple'* with Lydia, and teaches Lawrence a card trick – his first – using Top Trumps military planes. He also doesn't object when they jump on the sofa and throw the cushions at each other and onto the floor. When it's time to go, Alison gives Lydia a little purse with an Easter egg inside it, and Lawrence a chocolate hen to take home. But the rain has started so we can't go to the park. And Lawrence bursts into tears and turns his face to the wall in a sulk. Having taken a shine to Frank, he has clearly set his heart on going to the park with him.

Alison, having two Grown-up boys, doesn't bat an eye. But I am mortified, and demand he at least turn round and say Thank You for the lunch.

'If you don't say Thank You,' I say, 'you won't able to take home the chocolate hen.'

Lawrence doesn't reply.

'Say Thank You!'

Nothing.

'I'm really sorry . . .'

'It's OK. Don't worry!'

Eventually we get into the car, but Lydia has lost My Little Pony's tiara and Lawrence is still sobbing. I go back in the rain but can't find the tiara. We set off.

A few hundred yards down the road, Lawrence says, 'Frank said he'd take me to the park.'

It's like listening to some child brought up in an orphanage who's never had a dad.

I say, 'We've been over this. It's *raining*.' He continues to whine in the back.

I say to Peter, 'That was embarrassing. Couldn't you

have said something? Couldn't you at least have backed me up?'

'Oh, it's always about this, isn't it?'

'I think manners are important. It's just so depressing. Lawrence, for God's sake, Shut Up.'

Peter says, 'Just don't do this, OK?'

'But why? Why can't you tell them to say Thank You? Why is it always me?'

Lawrence says, 'Can you two just stop arguing?'

We go on like this for a few more minutes, then Peter pulls over, stops the car and gets out. It's still raining, but he turns a corner quickly and is gone.

Well, fine. He can go. I don't care. That's it. In fact, I'm glad. I get out, slam the door, shout, *'Fuck off!!!'* and get into the driver's seat.

Lydia is silent. Lawrence is still semi-crying. I berate him soundly for causing the argument between me and Peter, then, when I've calmed down a bit, explain I'm going to get out and see if he's round the corner, maybe waiting. Lawrence doesn't want me to.

'Don't go,' he pleads. 'It'll be like that time at the butcher's.'

The Time at the Butcher's is one of my Top Ten Worst Parenting Moments. I stopped there early one Saturday morning on the way to my mum's, thinking to bring her some dinner. The children wanted to stay in the car. But the queue was longer than I anticipated, and when it came to my turn, the guy went into the cold room for absolutely ages to get my meat. He must have thought I'd said, '*Haunch of pteranodon*' because it took a bloody long time. By the time I got back to the car, Lydia was fine but Lawrence was staring out of the back window, sobbing. He thought I wasn't coming back. I've berated myself over and over again for not going back out to the car to tell them, or to make them come into the shop and wait with me, but I didn't. I don't know why. And I feel absolutely terrible because ever since that day Lawrence has followed me – not all the time but sometimes – or, when I'm working, come up to check I'm still there. I'm pretty sure I've ruined his peace of mind, his security forever. And for what? Four venison steaks that I overcooked.

'It's OK,' I say. 'It won't be like the butcher's because I'm only going to peep round that corner and see if he's there. Why don't you come with me?'

Lydia doesn't want to come. So I lock her in and take Lawrence the three or so yards round the corner to where we can see down the road. Peter is standing in a bus shelter, looking the other way. I say to Lawrence, 'D'you want to get him?' But he is already coming towards us.

'Come on,' I say. 'You'll wait ages for a bus, and it's

raining.' Inwardly, I congratulate myself on my compassion, because, though I do not know it then, he has already taken a wrong turning in the car and has no idea where we are. He could well end up getting a bus to France. But he is not grateful.

'Just don't ever speak to me like that again,' he says, as he whisks the car keys out of my hand. 'And Lawrence is going in the front.' He picks up Lawrence and carries him to the car, where he is installed in my seat. I am demoted to the back, with Lydia, the tiaraless My Little Pony and the Cheestring wrappers.

We set off. After about half a mile I realize I don't recognize the shape of the road, the lack of green on one side where there should be green, or any of the shops.

'We're going the wrong way.'

'No, we're not.'

'Yes, we are. Look: that sign says Dartford. And the other places on there are Plumstead and Bexleyheath.'

'It's fine.'

'But we don't live in any of those places. We must be going the wrong way.'

I ask Lawrence to give me the map.

Peter says, 'I'm going to keep going.'

'Well, you're wrong. Look! There's a bus saying Greenwich, going the other way!'

'Anyway.'

'And there's one to Lewisham, for God's sake!'

There's a Streetcar Named Sanity as well, and that's *definitely* going the other way.

I open the *A–Z*, but there's just one problem. I can't read it.

'I can't read it. Pull over.'

'Give it to me.'

'Get Lawrence to do it.' Lawrence's eyesight is wonderful. He can read *Captain Underpants and the Big Bad Battle of the Bionic Booger Boy: The Night of the Nasty Nostril Nuggets* in the dark. Lydia can too, but her index capabilities are not so well honed.

What's that road over there? Get that and we can look it up.'

'Where?'

'There. No, *there*. No, *THERE*!'

We get the name of the road and Lawrence begins trying to find it in the index. He knows his alphabet, but I can see this is going to take a while. There are probably families where this would become a jolly adventure, an opportunity for everyone to map read and pull together. In our case, Peter and I want to kill each other, and Lawrence has forgotten how to find the letter N. If this were an episode of *Sesame Street*, it would be brought to you by the number four, the letter

N and the Marriage Guidance Council. And yes, I know they've changed their name to *Relationship Counselling Without Saying You Have to Be Married or Heterosexual or Anything*. On this wet, winter Sunday evening Marriage Guidance is what we need, from firm guiders who have the Answers. Instead we have an *A–Z* we can't read.

Nonetheless, we all pore over it. Well, I don't, having been relegated to the back. But Lawrence, after just fifteen minutes and lots of positive reinforcement from Peter, finds the road in the index and then the right square on the right page. I suffer a brief stab of guilt that we're not inviting Lydia to do it, since she's the one currently Doing Maps. But if we turned our family outings into coursework to support the curriculum, they'd become stressful. We've got the road name and the right square. There's just one problem. The road is so tiny, and the name so abbreviated, no one can read it, not even Lawrence. It's also on the join, thus proving my theory that everywhere you ever want to go in life is On the Join. Why can't we live our life squarely in the middle of the page, and not endlessly along what printers, appropriately, used to call the Gutter?

'Right!' says Peter. 'We'll just carry on.' He pulls out and resumes powering on towards Kent. The *A–Z* is thrown into the footwell.

'So what's the point of having a map, then? We are going the Wrong Way!'

'No, we're not. How could we have made a 180-degree turn?'

'I don't know how you do these things. It must be a kind of *gift*.'

Eventually I see a clear road sign, on the main road this time, which I can actually read on the map.

'According to this, we're on Crook Log Road, and we were on Park View Road, so therefore we are travelling *east*. We are also further away from home than when we began.' I pause, savouring my triumph. 'We need to turn round.'

Ah, the satisfaction!

But does he thank me? No! He merely turns off, turns round and gets back onto the main road, this time going the right way. When we're back in familiar territory, but still at least half an hour from home, I allow myself the pleasure of adding, 'Now we've hit the Sunday Traffic.'

We get home, children hungry and thirsty, adults glowering, an hour and a half after we set out. I go and check my emails, leaving Peter to put the children to bed. There's one from my sister, saying, '*Clocks forward tonight, don't forget!*' So that's one hour less to sort out my Life. Later, I dig my phone out and see a New Message.

'We are watching Casablanca *at 8.30 if you can get away. Sarah X.'* I look at my watch: *9.20.* Sarah only lives ten minutes away, so I could have made it: a film starring one of my favourite actors, with a friend whose company never fails to make me feel better. If I could have chosen the exact thing I would have most wanted to find on getting home, it would have been this. It would have blown away the poisonous feelings and made me optimistic again. It would have reminded me there are bigger issues in the world than my child not saying thank you for lunch. I can't believe I've missed it. It's so unfair, I feel like lying on the floor and sobbing. As I sit at my desk, wondering how on earth I'm going to stay married, there's a knock on the door.

'I thought you might like this.' Peter hands me a glass of wine.

'Oh! Thank you!'

'I'm about to watch *The Talented Mr Ripley*. Would you care to join me?'

We've seen it before, but he's our favourite psychopath.

This is one of Peter's skills. If he were the leader of the Shias or the Sunnis – just to name some current enemies at random – Iraq wouldn't be in the mess it's in. He'd just come in and say, 'Anyone for a bit of serial killing in Venice in fifties costumes?'

And they'd sit down, and get out the mint tea and falafel, and forget about who did what to whom under which dictatorship, and everything would be all right.

24 Phosphorus and Oxygen

I'm trying to work out whether Peter and I are more likely to stay together because of the children. At first I think, *Yes*, because every time I do think of leaving – I know I can't. But then I look at it the other way round. If I was able to shove off and have the odd night away, get some breathing space, would we get on better and therefore be less likely to split up? And now that he is 'differently employed', we see even more of each other. We're together, I realize, for about 90 per cent of our time. Hmm. This could prove to be about 30 per cent too much.

He asks me what the children said after he got out of the car, if they thought he'd left for good.

'No,' I admit, though I am tempted to say they did, to make him feel bad. 'They were quite worried when you went to Brighton for the night, though,' I add, so he doesn't go away completely guilt-free. This was when we'd had a row, and although we had got back on speaking terms – just – he stayed the night with friends.

Making people feel guilty is something adults do a lot, yet it's surely a rather babyish way to get what you want. Those ads placed by charities to raise aid money, for instance. The malnourished infant is meant to make you feel absolutely terrible – though not *so* terrible that you commit suicide, thus rendering yourself, as a source of income, completely useless. Those, and the adopt-a-child ones, pander to the Inner Toddler in all of us who'd like to Make the World Better by spending £10 a month on *one* child out of the millions who are suffering and dying – of diarrhoea, Aids and malaria – all the time. This is the equivalent of Lydia wanting to bandage up an injured worm that we saw on the pavement so that it could return to its vital work aerating the soil on the six-foot-wide grass patch by the traffic lights to help it stay green.

But everyone knows that the real reasons for all that death – civil war, for instance – are insoluble, and if they put that in the ads – *'Don't give: situation hopeless'* – they would feel ineffective. And feeling ineffective is not an empowering, adult way to feel.

And thinking about *this* reminds me of how Peter and I have always got on brilliantly when dealing with Big Crises, whereas we argue frequently and loudly over the small stuff, sometimes to the point of apparent no return.

We decide we need a device, a *cause*, to give ourselves a boost. We must, as Lawrence firmly tells me, 'Try to be nice to each other for a change.'

So we seek out something to inspire us. And we find it. Just as parents always feel hugely better when witnessing other people's children misbehaving, we are massively buoyed up by the sight of other adults doing the same.

One Saturday, Peter comes back from a party he's taken Lawrence to, with a good story of Grown-ups gone wrong.

'The party was in the church hall, and a clown had been hired,' he explains. He notes the look on my face, as he knows how I feel about clowns. 'But the children were quite rowdy – 30 seven-year-old boys all full of sugar and starting to break loose . . .'

'A reminder, if one were needed, of why we don't do big parties.'

'Quite. Gradually it became apparent that the clown had lost control of his audience. They were running amok, basically, while he attempted to carry on tying balloons. So the birthday boy's father sacked him.'

'In the middle of the party?'

'Yep. Not only that, he persuaded two other parents to take over with him.'

'With the balloons?'

'No, but they started telling jokes, and slightly calmed the situation down.'

'Phew.'

'But the clown wasn't happy. He started remonstrating with the dad, and an argument broke out.'

'Had he not got paid?'

'I don't know. Shut up. He raised his voice, and the dad raised his voice, and eventually we were all listening to a man in a red nose and long shoes saying, "You're being completely unreasonable!"'

I like this story, and Peter and I agree that if we can only find enough examples of adults behaving worse than we do, it will be immensely bonding and almost certainly save the marriage. I've always wished I could find a way to spy on other people when they're alone, to see if their relationships are any calmer, or if we really are the worst. My mother says it's the ones who say '*Never a cross word in thirty years*' who end up with an axe in their heads. I do hope so.

And I'm glad to say, once I start focusing, that I find more than enough examples. One day on the way to pick-up, I realize I am walking behind a couple at school who, though I've never actually met them, I recognize as being active in the PTA. The husband is vicarish of demeanour, while the wife wears clothes that are so awful, she has to be an absolutely lovely human being. They don't see me, and to start with I'm not eavesdropping, but as I speed up on the assumption that without even checking my watch I must be late, I hear her tell him:

'You make me *sick*!' The level of contempt, and the force with which the words come spitting out of her mouth, shock me so much that instead of staying on their tails I involuntarily slacken my pace, allowing me to remain undetected and out of earshot when I ring Peter with the good news.

'So, do you think arguing is a healthy thing in a marriage, or not?'

'It wasn't in your parents' case, was it?' he says.

He points this out from time to time because he thinks I advocate yelling and breaking things as a life-style choice.

'No, but – yes. Because if they hadn't – if they hadn't been allowed to divorce for some reason – it would have been worse.' My sister dedicated one of her books to them, as a couple who 'split up for the sake of the children'. People never get credit for that.

'So you're saying all that shouting you had to listen to was good?'

'You know perfectly well I'm not. I'm saying they were two fascinating people who probably shouldn't have married each other.' Like phosphorus and oxygen, they were stable on their own but once together, blew up. Even as a child I remember noticing that they got on far better once they were apart.

'And anyhow, I suppose your parents agreed about everything, all the time?'

Though they're both dead, he generously allows me the odd bit of low-level criticism.

'Of course not. But I think they didn't tend to discuss the things they didn't agree on. For example, my father wasn't at all religious, and when my mother taught me the Lord's Prayer, I realized afterwards that he didn't approve.'

'Phew! Is that as bad as it got?'

He gives me a look.

'Sorry.'

'I just hate it when we fight,' he says finally.

'Well, why don't you just agree with me, then? And we need never fight again.'

Ha ha. But soon after this, good news! With no prompting from us, Lawrence reports that a boy he's recently been to play with, a very polite child, has a family who are, in fact, quite rude.

'They're really horrible to each other,' he says.

This is *great*.

'What, worse than us??'

'Oh, much worse.'

'Why? How? What do they say to each other?'

'I don't know! Leave me alone. I'm on the computer.'

All attempts to extract the gory details are defeated, so I talk it over with my new friend Sarah who, like me, has always wanted a family that sits round the table talking and eating happily, in what we both imagine as an Italian sort of way, and who, like me, finds this a challenge, though whereas we sit round the table, to use Lydia's phrase, getting *shirty*, her lot are more inclined to just wander off. She's even married to someone with Italian forebears and it still hasn't produced the ideal result, although they do make ice cream for a living which is the ultimate compensation for anything.

'These families who appear to behave really nicely,' I ask her. 'Are they behaving nicely because order has been imposed from above – as happened with Yugoslavia – or is it because they've got so little to talk about, an argument can't arise?'

'Or are they just – you know, good?'

This is her slight weakness: a tendency to think the best of people. It could get in the way of our friendship. After all, I've got a husband like that already; I don't need it in a friend. I need someone who's going to play to my irrational prejudices and, if possible, extend them; who will smoke out the bees in my bonnet, not pacify them with nectar.

But then I realize that for Peter and me, one of the main causes of conflict is actually the different ways in which we handle conflict. When something bad happens, my instinct is to Spring into Action, while his is to Do Bugger All. (He is reading this over my shoulder and claims that he is not Doing Bugger All in those situations, but Deciding his Strategy. Oddly, they look the same.) As far as I can see, his deliberations are designed to find reasons for Not Reacting, which he can get away with because he knows I'm going to React for us both.

I first had an inkling of this when he was staying over at my flat one night when we first got together. The people upstairs were given to drinking, smoking and generally getting out of it, which for some reason affected their hearing, so they used to turn the TV up REALLY LOUD. One night I'd had enough – we were in bed at 11.30 p.m. trying to get to sleep, for God's sake – so I said to Peter, 'This is ridiculous. Can't you go up and ask them to turn it down?' I wasn't putting him in danger, by the way; they weren't psychopaths

272

who turn the music up and then go out for the night, just old farts who drank too much. And he said, in a tone with which I was to become extremely familiar over the next seventeen years: 'They'll probably stop in a minute.'

I mean, you can see my point. It's very very ANNOYING. Yet he continues to justify it.

'Imagine if Churchill had taken that tack over Czechoslovakia,' I say triumphantly. 'Mmm?'

'Well, actually Churchill didn't, because when the Germans annexed the Sudetenland, he wasn't running the country.'

'I knew that.'

'It was Chamberlain. And he didn't declare war for another year, which was a Good Thing.'

'Why?'

'Because we weren't prepared. If we'd gone to war then, there's a very good chance we'd have been beaten. So that just goes to show.'

'Well, all right. It does in that instance.'

'You see?'

'It's hardly the same thing.'

'Yes, it is. Same principle. You just think if someone doesn't lose their temper, they're not being strong and effective.'

'I don't. You think if someone *does* lose their temper, they're not being strong and effective. Which is just – absurd.'

'No, it isn't.'

'It is! I overheard you telling off that man at work on the phone that time, and you were brilliant.'

Here I suddenly deploy my strategy of, in the middle of a disagreement, unexpectedly paying the other person a compliment. Hah! Even better, acceptance of the compliment means they accept my point of view. Hah! Hah!

'Well – I don't believe you.'

Oh.

'Well – you should.'

He pours us some more wine and warms to his theme.

'And another thing, when Dee had that weird guy hanging around at the bottom of the garden . . .'

Dee was my American predecessor. He lived with her in Washington. She was dark, beautiful and high-powered; he goes for a type.

'All the blokes in the house wanted to get out there and go for him. And I said, "Don't be silly: this is America. He might be carrying a sub-machine gun."'

'And was he?'

'No. But I persuaded them to hold back, and he Went Away. And *then* . . .'

The conversation has somehow gone from a persuasive argument in favour of intervention – well, I say it's persuasive – to Perfect Peter's Greatest Hits. How have I let this happen?

'There was that guy, Greg, who lived upstairs. Dee was quite friendly with him, and then she wasn't, and he starting behaving quite scarily. He threw a lighted cigarette onto her bed.'

'While she was in it?'

'Yeah. She was awake, though.'

'So *that's* all right.'

'D'you want me to tell you or not? And I told her she had to go upstairs and talk to him.'

'Didn't you think he might be dangerous?'

'I made a judgement, that he'd listen to reason.'

It's when he's at his most social-workery that I want to flick gravy at him.

'Yeah, right. And?'

'She did go up and talk to him, and we never had any more trouble.'

Oh.

'She was lucky. Anyhow, you don't know what she said up there.'

'And I'll tell you another thing. He'd abandoned his studies and was lying around watching TV and smoking dope all day, and after that he went back to law school.'

'Oh, for God's sake.'

'It's true!'

'And what is he now, Chief Counsel to the White House? Head of the UN?'

'I dunno. I might Google him, actually . . .'

It doesn't end there. That night at dinner, he says:

'And what about the Scary Builder?'

'Oh, come on! What man wouldn't protect his wife from some chemically enhanced . . . weirdo with a chisel?'

'He didn't have a chisel.'

'He did in his toolbox.'

'He was a *builder*.'

'If you remember, he started staring at me in this really weird way. So I started stacking the dishes to take my mind off it. And then he told me off for not looking at him when he was speaking to me, so I hid in the bedroom and rang you.'

'Yeah, and I Dealt With It.'

'Well, bully for you! Even Gareth Hill did that.'

Gareth Hill is our barometer of Unsupportive Husbandness. His wife was alone in the house with a scary builder and he came home and sacked him. It was a relief to all of us because usually whatever his wife says he automatically discounts. If she was struck by lightning in the middle of her own kitchen, it would be her fault.

'And it wasn't as though you dashed right over. I was up there for two hours.'

'I had a *job*.'

'Those were the days.'

That night in bed, I say, 'The people opposite have got their million-watt light on again. It's shining right in here.'

And he says: 'It's fine. It'll go off in a minute.'

And it does.

25 A Chemical Imbalance

When adults argue, it appears that they're supposed to leave out feelings as somehow invalid. But if I think something's worth arguing about, it's usually because I mind about it, and when I mind about something, I get emotional. So there we are. Actually, I'm not sure this is a Grown-up thing as opposed to a Male Thing. Whenever I disagree with men they usually accuse me of arguing 'emotionally', and seem to think they can, because of that, discount what I'm actually saying. (They also often say, when I disagree with them: 'You're missing the point.') I've been 'disqualified' on those grounds countless times. But that's ridiculous, like saying you don't like chicken if it's served on a red plate. In other words, it's childish. So they're the babies, not me.

It follows from that position that ideas are superior to feelings, which is just *dumb*. If ideas were all that counted you'd never be allowed to have children, because you hadn't come up with a proper *reason*. No one gets pregnant because they want to restore the pensions-creating capacity of the income tax base. And how can you explain falling in love? So as a dialectical position, it's bollocks. As for whether more people since the dawn of Time have killed each other over ideas or feelings, well, just look at the papers.

Just by way of illustration, see what you think of these two arguments, both with men in Very Grown-up jobs. The first was with a psychiatrist attached to one of the large London hospitals.

HIM: 'Depression is the same as heart disease or diabetes: you take your medication for life and that's that.'

ME: 'Depression is very much *not* like diabetes. It can stem from something that's happened to you, or years of prolonged sadness, anger – all sorts of things.'

HIM: 'No, it's a chemical imbalance in the brain.'

ME: 'That's never been proven.'

'Yes, it has.'

'No, it hasn't.'

'Yes, it has!'

'It really hasn't!'

I think you can see here how I'm able to build an argument against someone far more educated and qualified by repeating the same thing over and over again.

'It's a fact. It just is.'

279

Across the table I could see Peter mouthing *No* at me. I ignored him.

'Look. I was depressed for a number of years. I had therapy, which is admittedly slow and expensive, and I got better. I'm not depressed any more.'

'No no no. That's not the case.'

'What do you mean, Not the Case? Here I am, the Living Proof.'

'Not at all. One of two things happened. Either you were never depressed in the first place—'

'Trust me.'

'Or you would have got better anyway.'

'Well, you can't have it both ways.'

'Therapy is nonsense! Depression is a chemical imbalance in the brain.'

'Really? Do you ever talk to your patients? Ask them why they feel that way?'

'That's not the point.'

'You're condemning them to a life on medication without even asking them why they feel that way.'

HIM [*lip quivering now*]: 'But I'm an Expert in this field!'

ME [*heart beating*]: 'Well, you're still Wrong.'

He then sulked, presumably the result of a chemical imbalance, until his wife took him home.

*

And here's the second, more recent dispute I had, with a man I met at a dinner party who was working in Downing Street at the time Tony Blair announced we were invading Iraq.

ME: 'Was there a moment, at any time during the period before this, when anyone there asked: *'Is there any chance that our actions here may result in trouble later on?'*, e.g. London Underground stations and buses being bombed?'

HIM: 'Oh, you're saying the War caused the July 7 bombings. Well, that's absurd.'

ME: 'I didn't say that. All I said was, did anyone ask the question?'

'That's such a typical media position, blaming it on that.'

'I didn't say that. All I said was, did anyone ask the question?'

'That's so typical! The media always do that.'

'But that's not what I said. I asked if anyone asked the question.'

'You media people are all alike.'

HOST: 'Coffee, anyone?'

And which style of arguing is more 'Grown-up'? Answer: neither. Peter's is the most Grown-up, according to him, because he never argues in these situations at all, but sits nicely and quietly, says 'Thank you for having me,' and always gets asked back.

Sometimes, of course, you don't *want* to be asked back.

I went to a dinner party once where everyone was talking about dogs – dogs they owned, dogs their friends owned, dogs with four legs, and so on. As we came in, the owner of the house said, with a nervous giggle: 'This is Stephanie. She hates dogs!'

No one laughed, or smiled. The temperature in the room fell about forty degrees. To be fair to her, it was meant partly as a joke, a reference, I assumed, to my strange penchant for not wanting my coat stamped with muddy pawprints and my tights shredded whenever I came in the door. The woman next to me was describing the trauma of how she'd gone to buy puppies from some people in the country.

'They were practically gypsies!' she said, appalled. She had that sort of hair that doesn't move, like Playmobil hair, that you imagine being able to snap on and off.

'Oh,' I said. 'And what were they actually *like*?'

'They were . . .' and here she struggled, *'fat.'*

I looked around the room. *You're frankly no Audrey Hepburn yourself, Mrs*, I thought. Peter raised his eyebrows at me, but no one else reacted at all. Then, because one of the guests was a lawyer, someone brought up the story in the paper that the police had been asking banks for the personal details of men whose credit cards had been used to pay for child pornography. And the banks had refused.

It went a bit quiet. The lawyer said, 'Things in these cases aren't always what they seem,' but then wouldn't say any more, which was frustrating.

'What worries me,' I said, 'are the shops which sell sexually provocative clothes for little girls.' It was particularly bad at the time – tankinis for four-year-olds and so on, though we currently have 'Funky Friends' stationery for Lydia's age group that says '*I'm super hot*'. Note to the manufacturers of this stuff: do you know what '*hot*' actually means?

I continued: 'If you go to Next, for example . . .' Suddenly Snap-on Hair went for me.

'Well, I don't!' she barked. 'My daughter and I don't go there!'

'I just mean for example Next,' I said. 'If you go in there—'

'Well, I don't!' she barked again. 'I don't! *OK*??'

Everyone stopped talking. Did she work for Next? Not in that padded waistcoat. Had I exposed the dark underbelly of something she wanted kept hidden? I didn't know, but the next thing was, I found myself in the bathroom, crying. Forty years old! Why couldn't I just shrug it off? I felt very, very small. I wanted to ring my dad, except I didn't have my phone in there and anyway he was dead. I knew what he would have said: *'Frightful cow! But you're an adult now. You don't have to go to school tomorrow and sit next to her.'* I thought of waiting until Peter realized I'd gone, and came to find me. But he probably wouldn't notice for ages; I might have to stay in there all night. I blew my nose and sat gazing at their washing machine for a while, watching the games kit going round.

Eventually I tiptoed to the door, slipped out and walked home. Vicky, our babysitter, listened to my plan without betraying any suspicion on her part that I might have gone mad.

'Some awful woman's just shouted at me,' I told her. 'I can't bear going back there. So I'm going to go back and tell them you've got to get home immediately, because, er, you've got to revise. And I'll have to come back here and stay with the kids. OK?'

'O-kay . . .' She gathered her things slowly, one eye on me, one on the door, like someone trying not to inflame the mad person even more.

Maybe adults 'rationalize' themselves off the point. The next day, coming back from shopping, Lawrence told me: 'We must get some chocolate cake.'

And I said, 'Why must we?'

'Because otherwise . . . we won't have any chocolate cake!'

It is the purest logic I've ever heard.

26 From Here to Maturity

The point has come where everyone's sick of it, even me. Pleading hasn't worked, nor has asking nicely. So we've got a Swearing Jar.

And although I make no pretence of being well behaved or Good – at anything much – this is embarrassing, an admission that my bad language is out of control. In the car, I agree with them that it's unacceptable.

'That's your side, that's MY side! Move OVER, you twat!'

'Mummy!'

'Swear jar 10p!'

'Shit, sorry.'

'Swear jar 10p!'

'Mummy! Don't *say* that!'

'Sorry. Hey, if you can't use an indicator . . . You fuckwit!'

'MUMMY!'
'Sorry.'
'Swear jar 10p!'

And so it goes on. The thing is, I never had it till I had the children. No, shit – wait. I did. It's just that now I'm under more strain. And I'm surrounded by meticulous moral Munchkins who never fail to pull me up on it every time.

So every time I swear I'm going to put 10p in the jar. When I suggested it to Lawrence, his eyes lit up. I said he and Lydia could share it. At the rate I'm going they'll be spending next Christmas in Barbados.

It must be wonderful always to say the right thing. Or even sometimes. Claire and I were at a party once, and we got talking to two men. One was considerably older than the other – I assumed father and son – and they were both quite charming. After a while, I noticed that while the younger one mentioned Croatia several times, the older one didn't.

'Did you not grow up there with him, then?' I said.

The older one frowned.

'Why? Did you think we were related?'

I did of course, so I said, 'Well, I didn't think you were *dating*!!'

There was then a very long pause, until Claire said quietly, 'I think they *are* . . .'

I apologized – quite a lot – and since, as Claire said, they realized I was stupid rather than offensive, the evening ended on a positive note.

Since then I have tried even harder to say the right thing, to be In Control. But life, or my take on it, defeats me. It's not always my fault. As with foreign phrase books, it's never the things you're prepared for in life that actually happen. When your relationship goes belly-up on holiday, you don't want *My room is too hot/too cold*; you want *My husband is too mean/too dismissive/ too unfaithful/too pissed.*

It's nearly teatime. The children are doing their homework. The phone rings. I answer it. On the line is my friend Gill, whom I haven't seen for a long time. Too long.

'Hey! How's it going?' And straight away I know.

'I'm sorry we haven't been in touch. Tim's – got cancer.'

'Oh, no . . .'

'Yeah.'

'When did this – when did you know?'

She breathes out. I can feel her building up to telling me about it, the diagnosis, the history. I can also feel, through the floor, the rumble of tiny feet.

'I haven't seen you – I mean, I assumed you were fine. Oh God, I'm so sorry.'

Suddenly Lawrence is in my face.

'Lydia's taken the red pencil.'

I cover the phone and mouth, *'NOT NOW.'*

'We've got loads of red pencils. Get another one!'

'Make her give it back. I was using it first!'

'Well, then tell Lydia to get another one.'

I shut the door on them and go and sit on the stairs.

'When did you find out?'

'He went to the doctor's with these pains – you know. And the doctor said—'

The kitchen door is flung open and they both charge up the stairs.

'Mummy! Lawrence threw Twilight at me!'

Twilight is Lydia's pet unicorn. She has not been bred to cope with domestic violence.

'Make her give me the red pencil!'

'OK. Sssh!'

'Mummy said you had to give me the red pencil!'

'Tell him off!!'

'Lawrence! Say sorry!' I wave him away.

Gill says, 'I'm sorry – I've rung at a bad time.'

'No! No! Don't be – I'm really sorry. What did the doctor say?'

'She said it was nothing. And of course it wasn't nothing. It was a tumour in his stomach.'

'No . . . Oh, Gill.'

Lydia is standing over me, arms folded, with a scowl.

'Mummy! Why aren't you telling Lawrence off?!'

I mouth, '*NOT NOW. ANY TIME BUT NOW.*' Then I whisper, '*PLEASE GO AWAY.*'

'Don't tell me to Go Away!'

'Oh, *please* . . .'

'They say it's now a matter of weeks.'

'Can you just – shove off back to what you were doing? *PLEASE?*'

I scramble up the rest of the stairs, pointing desperately at the phone. Those people who do Sign Language With Your Baby, haven't they got something for: '*My friend's husband is dying here. Go and sort it out yourselves or I will shove the bloody red pencil in the bin?*'

'Please go back in the kitchen? *Please?*' I say to Gill, 'What can I do?'

'We're just, you know.'

I know what she's trying to say. I want to reach out to her down the phone and make it all better. I want to—

'MUMMY! WHERE ARE YOU??!'

I am sitting in the bedroom under the ironing board.

'Would you like me to come over?'

'Well, we're sort of taking it one day at a time really.'

The door handle is being rattled. I don't know if you've ever tried to hassle the wife of a cancer patient to get her diary before your warring children wrest the door open, but if there's a 'right' way of doing it, do let me know.

My mother once had lessons in how to say the right thing. Or rather, how to say what you want – something even some big mouths like me have trouble with. This was an Assertion Training Group in the consciousness-raising seventies, and being teenagers at the time, my sister and I were merciless in our observations.

'Oh-oh, it's the Assertion Group at the door again!'

'How do you know?'

'You can't hear the bell properly, because they can't press it firmly enough.'

'Oh, that's so amusing!'

Integral to the training was that you had to be totally direct about your needs. For example, you weren't allowed to lie when Saying No; you always had to say, '*No, I do not wish to do that*,' because making excuses was considered to be little better than saying Yes to something you didn't want.

I always lie. Mind you, it's become easier since I realized that people on the other end of the phone can't see into my diary – a hangover from being at one of those schools where the Head always seemed to know what you were up to.

The trouble is, we all have different expectations. When I pointed out to Lawrence that the reason a wheel had come off his Jaguar was because he'd thrown it, I added, in a rather feeble attempt to discourage him: 'Big boys don't do that.'

And he replied: 'But I'm two.'

At least he knew how old he was. I was at a party recently and went to the bathroom for a wee. After I'd been in there about ninety seconds, a woman came and tried the door. I called out that there was someone in there, but she tried it again. I told her again. As I started to wash my hands, a second person evidently joined her out there, and asked if she'd been waiting long. So she started rattling the door handle and called out: 'Yes, I have! Someone should tell that person to come out!'

I flung open the door, glared at her – in a very mature way – and flounced off. You may *look* forty, whoever you are, but your Inner Age is about two. Next time, try saying: 'I'm a pissed old boiler with a wrecked pelvic floor who's going to wet herself.' But even then, I still say it's about time you learned to take turns.

Whenever I meet people, I find new and fascinating discrepancies between their expectations and my own. I thought this stuff was supposed to be ironed out in nursery.

For example, I went out for a night a while back with a couple of women I didn't know very well. We met up at the house of one of them, Anne. As we were deciding whose car to go in, she suddenly said, 'Steph can drive me home.'

And I thought, *Don't be mad. It's miles away and in the wrong direction!* But I let her boss me into it because her husband had left her and mine hadn't, and I felt guilty. And, at around midnight, as I eventually turned out of her street and shot onto a dual carriageway going the wrong way in an area I didn't know, I thought: *I'd have probably left her too.*

How much ought we to be able to expect from others? When Lydia, then four, admitted to having lost my pen, Lawrence – aged five – snapped at me: 'Well? D'you still love her??!'

I remember having over a girl Lydia was desperate to have to stay the night. After about an hour, she totally refused to play with her, putting me in the unenviable position of saying, 'Lydia! Play with your friend right now!' while Lydia answered, within earshot, 'But she's being really annoying!'

We think of this as solely childish behaviour, but it isn't. I've known at least two serially unfaithful men – nothing to do with me, thank you very much – to whom I wanted to say, 'Go on! That's your wife there. No, *there*. Play with her, not them. You married her. Well, I'm sorry. You can't chop and change now.'

Whether you can do it depends entirely on your expectations. Daily Life in our house often resembles *Adam's Rib*, the Katharine Hepburn–Spencer Tracy film about two lawyers on opposing sides of a case who are married to each other. Mind you, they had a better script. Remember those cartoons, *Love Is* . . . 'Love Is . . . giving her your last sweet' or whatever? Maybe they should do a slightly more adult version. *Being a Grown-up Is* . . . knowing when to shut the fuck up.

And sorry, Erich Segal: love *doesn't* mean never having to say you're sorry. That's just where you're wrong.

Lawrence once said to Katarina: 'I want to say sorry about the smackings.'

We were having dinner at the time. I said, 'What smackings?'

He'd apparently hit her earlier in the day, and wanted

to apologize. He was three months short of his third birthday. I thought, *I must remember to learn how to do that.*

Unless you live all your life alone, waiting for The One, you come to the dazzling realization after the age of about twenty that everyone does *something* that becomes fantastically irritating if you live with them long enough. If they throw the stereo across the room because their dinner isn't hot enough, you can complain. Or, better still, leave. But snoring, leaving the bread unwrapped after making a piece of toast so it dries up every time – *yes, you* – or going to sleep during *Green Wing* and waking up in the middle of *My Name is Earl* mumbling, 'Why have they become American?' That you just have to suffer.

Crosby, Stills & Nash once sang, *If you can't be with the one you love, love the one you're with*, which I think is a good philosophy. On the other hand, it's the sort of thing your mother says when you've just been passed over by the class hunk, but the one with smelly armpits and dandruff is just desperate to take you to see *Blood and Entrails IV*.

In *When Harry Met Sally*, Carrie Fisher says to Bruno Kirby, 'Tell me I'll never have to be Out There again.'

And Peter and I have agreed that if at all possible, we will at least try to save each other from that.

The last time I was chucked, it was such an unpleasant experience I can only assume it was character forming. Actually, in my case, I had to chuck myself. Tom was so unable to communicate whatever was bothering him that he gradually spoke to me less and less. It took a month of sitting there practically in silence before I became so miserable and lonely I rang him one night and, in effect, forced him to finish with me. How long would he have gone on otherwise, barely speaking? Another month? A year? Twenty? Actually, come to think of it, I have a cousin like that. He's said nothing to his wife since 1964. Now I'd take the initiative sooner. I'd give Tom till lunchtime, then say, *'I've put back your Elmore Leonard books. Thanks for all the salads – I'm off.'* Except I'd try to sound less like the dolphins quoted in the title of that Douglas Adams book, *So Long, and Thanks for All the Fish*. Fair dos, though; the salads were good. And possibly if I'd been forty-three instead of twenty-three, I wouldn't have pleaded, 'But you said you loved me!'

And maybe if he hadn't been such an arsehole, he wouldn't have said, 'No, I didn't.'

Now, every time I think of him, I feel deeply grateful he let me make him chuck me.

*

So have I learned anything? I suppose each time we have to manage a loss is a staging post on the way to some kind of Maturity – assuming that's a destination at all, and not a journey with one of those rail companies which plasters its trains with slogans like *Moving You Forward!* while sending you off late, overcharged and badly fed. After all, when you look at what awaits you at the end of it all, you should surely get *some* kind of reward for having matured, or even just lasted a fair old while. But you don't.

'Well, here I am – all Grown-up! What do I get?'

'Death.'

'But that's not fair!'

'Ah, but you said you were a Grown-up. That means knowing Life is Unfair and Accepting it.'

'Sob!'

'Come on, now. Don't be a baby.'

'You bastards!'

27 Monsters Inc

While I'm trying to pin down once and for all what constitutes an adult, something I read by Eleanor Roosevelt pops back into my mind.

'*No one can make you feel inferior without your consent,*' she said, which I think was brilliant – or as brilliant as anything can be, said by someone from a country that until 150 years ago had slaves. Then I come across two articles in the same edition of the same paper which seemed to illustrate it exactly.

The first piece is about a lovely-looking, very tall girl, over six foot but aged only thirteen, who is being bullied at school. She is evidently middle class and accomplished, and while height is clearly an Issue, background may be part of it too. She's been picked on more and more; now her mother is keeping her at home. The second piece, a few pages further on, is also about an unusually tall girl. Same height as the other, in fact. But here's the interesting part. She's being interviewed because she can't find any shoes. She's not nearly as pretty as the first one – she's even overweight as well as 'too tall'. Yet there's no mention of any problem at school.

Same 'problem': two different realities.

So can you, to use one of Peter's favourite phrases, *decide* not to be bullied? Being bullied at school was one thing – as Donald Rumsfeld would say, stuff that shouldn't happen, happens – but when you're a Grown-up, you've outgrown all that. There are no more school bullies, right?

When I was twenty-five, I got my dream job: a page of my own, in a paper, and a desk to use three days a week. I loved it, most of all because the people were great. Well, except for one: Tony.

'What happened with him?' asks Peter. The irony is, I quite liked the guy.

'We got on fine to start with. But he had a bit of a thing for me and started sending me notes and so on. He worked in another department then. I told another bloke in the same office, who was sort of egging me on basically, that I couldn't possibly do anything with Tony because (a) he didn't really know me, he was just in love with the idea of it, and (b) he was married.'

'And then?'

'And then Tony got promoted and became my editor. And the other bloke, who was a much worse gossip than I'd realized, had clearly told him he didn't stand a chance with me or words to that effect, because he refused to have anything to do with me.'

'While being your editor?'

'Yeah. He wouldn't speak to me or look at me – at all.'

'Did you think of going to a Higher Authority?'

'What could I have said? "I'm not being Sexually Harassed?" He wasn't touching me up, he wasn't chasing me round the desk. He basically wasn't doing anything you could actually accuse him of.'

'Except making your life a misery.'

'Yeah. At meetings, with a dozen people in the room, he'd refer to me in the third person or ignore me altogether. And my desk was right outside his office, so I could hear him shouting at other people, calling them cunts and so on as well, and throwing their work on the floor.'

'Funnily enough, mine did that.'

We'll come to him shortly.

'I think he thought it was macho or something. So anyway, because I loved that job so much, I put up with it for two months. Then one day I went down to Mum's and just cried all over her. I so wanted someone to say it was OK to leave.'

'And did she?'

'Of course. It was such a relief. But awful, because I'd been earning good money for the first time ever.'

'Hmm.'

'Once I'd decided, though, I felt so much better. I went back – Lucy, the secretary, said I looked really strange when I came in, sort of eerily calm. She asked if I was all right. And I went into Tony's office; he still wouldn't look at me. My contract was still in his drawer – he hadn't renewed it. So I didn't have to give notice. I just said, "I can't do this any more. I'm going."'

'And what did he say?'

'He didn't seem surprised. He just said, "So you're not going to Sheffield, then?" Because he had some bizarre idea he wanted me to cover the Snooker Championships. And I said No. And that was it. I walked out. Floated. It felt fantastic.'

'I can imagine.'

'Not least not having to cover the Snooker Championships. But I didn't have a mortgage, remember. Or kids, or a car – or anything. So I wasn't a Grown-up in that sense at all. It was easy.'

'But you took control.'

'I suppose. But I didn't bide my time the way you did.'

'Yeah, well.'

Peter, when it happened to him, thought it all through and planned when and how to leave.

'And you *did* have kids, a car and a mortgage. And me.'

'I had to keep you in wine.'

'I've just realized something.'

'What?'

'I don't hate him. I don't even feel angry.'

'*Whoo-ooh!* Maybe you are a Grown-up and don't realize it.'

'Hah! I'll tell you what, though.'

'What?'

'I sort of want to bump into him somewhere, just so I can show I've Moved On. Just say, "Oh, hi – how are you?" very casually, moments before driving off in a very expensive car, or hearing my name called to accept an award.'

Very mature. Even though my own story disproves it, I've always believed that some people are natural victims. It somehow seems easier that way. But it's bollocks. I'm not. Peter's not. If anything, he has a talent for not winding people up – people who aren't me, at any rate. But one day, also in a job he loved, he got a new boss and was completely unprepared for what came next.

'It was as if suddenly we were in a scary, public

school type environment, like the film *If*. With a great big school bully who was totally out of control. I realized that the clothes, the reading glasses, the brogues – the whole uniform of adulthood – was just that; underneath he hadn't moved on. He was still the school bully.'

'Had he been, when he was young, do you think?'

'Well, people who "go bad" aren't nice, well-balanced human beings until the age of thirty-five, are they?' he says. 'They don't suddenly change.'

Peter wasn't the only target. The men got shouted at and the women groped.

'He'd suddenly lose his temper and march out of the room, swearing. Or burst into your office shouting "*Fucking idiot!*" about someone else.'

Peter responded in a very calm, adult way, talking to the HR department and so on.

'Nothing happened. They were too scared of him.'

In the end, Peter bided his time until he got offered another job.

'I don't really want to punish him any more,' he says.

'Don't you?' I say. 'I do.'

Revenge is not at *all* Grown-up – except in Albania, where you do it for two years instead of National Service.

'If anything I feel sorry for him.'

'Oh, come on.'

'Yes, because something hideous must have happened to make him so fucked up.'

We watched a documentary once about people in America who campaign against the death penalty, but specifically people who've had a loved one murdered. That's pretty Grown-up, isn't it? Being able not only to forgive, but to work to save the guilty from the ultimate punishment.

'I can't imagine being able to do that,' he says. 'I can more identify with the vicar whose daughter was blown up on July 7, who can't preach forgiveness anymore.'

'Yeah. But at least a campaign is somewhere to put all the energy that would go on anger.'

'If you could gather up all the energy *you've* spent on that over the years, we wouldn't need wind farms.'

'In fact, why not get all the angry people together and do like *Monsters Inc.*?'

'You wouldn't need the monsters. Parents could just come in and shout at their kids to get back into bed or stop fighting or whatever, and do it that way.'

Peter has solved how to fund the Bad Mothers Club for the next millennium: we'll go into electricity.

Great. But what I don't understand is why I don't feel angry about the dream job I gave up, and *am* constantly annoyed about things like the nightmare junction at the bottom of our road.

'Why don't I mind having given it up?'

'It was nearly twenty years ago,' Peter points out.

'I know! But look at that bloke we met who was still pissed off about his son not getting into the football team. This was three years after he left the school!'

'So?'

'So – we'd say that's far less important. You can't always tell what people are going to hang onto. Or resent.'

'I think it's all about Taking Control,' Peter says. 'Like you did with Harriman Road.'

In *Confessions of a Bad Mother* I wrote about the day we moved house. But I didn't say why we moved.

When Lawrence and Lydia were still babies, and we knew we were going to want to move to a bigger house at some point, we met some friends of friends who were emigrating. And we ended up buying their house. It had everything: a big garden, a conservatory, a garage and even a workshop – something Peter had wanted all his life. Oh yes, and an Aga. The minute we saw it, we were both deep in our respective fantasies, him sawing and nailing in the workshop, and me sipping wine and dispensing *bon mots* in the conservatory. We'd hold great parties. The place would be filled with lights, music and laughing, happy people. It would all be wonderful.

The Friday of the week we moved in, we were woken by sirens, followed by the sound of a crash. We rushed to the window; a police car had hit another car, on the roundabout outside. Did I mention there was a round-about? Suddenly there were sirens – it seemed constantly. It was so bad we moved out of our bedroom and into the little spare room high up at the back.

Then, about another week later, I found some kids in the front garden.

'Can I help you?' I said stiffly, in my Adult Voice. There was something not right about them. They weren't at all embarrassed or sorry or scared.

'We're looking for Number 30 – no, 40!' they said, not even trying to lie convincingly.

'Well, this is Number 3, so it's obviously not near here, is it?' I said. Then I noticed the silver packets. They seemed to be playing with them, throwing them over the wall and retrieving them. I'd dated an ex-junkie once, but this completely freaked me out. I got the impression they'd leave when they felt like it. It was like a recurring nightmare I'd had in the past, about coming home to find other people living in my flat. I stood my ground, kept it very low-key, and they wandered off.

Then at about five one Sunday morning I got up to give Lawrence a bottle and saw a man – in the back garden this time – coming towards the house. He looked up, saw me at the window, and disappeared over the garden wall. Peter recovered quite swiftly from the feeling of being invaded, but I felt very exposed. I said, 'I have a bad feeling about this place.'

He said: 'I'll put up a higher trellis.'

He put up a higher trellis, and fixed the drainpipe that the man had pulled down, and arranged the climbing roses over it. Then one morning a policeman came to the door and said, 'I'm afraid we have to evacuate you. There's a suspect bag on top of your wall, and it may be a bomb.'

There had just been a bomb in Brixton, leaving many injured, and another at a gay pub in Soho, killing three. Had someone panicked and left a bomb on our wall? I grabbed Lydia – Lawrence was at the childminder's – and walked quickly down the road. The police put tape all round the house and, after about four hours, announced that they had removed the bag; it contained stolen car radios.

A friend came to stay, in our basement room. She said, 'I don't want to make you nervous or anything, but last night there was someone outside, by the window. Sort of casing the joint. Being from Belfast,' she added, 'I'm not bothered. But I thought you should know.'

I started lying awake at night, listening for suspect noises and imagining what I'd do if we were burgled and/or attacked. Then we really did hear noises.

'There's something scuttling about up there in the ceiling,' I told Peter, and for once he said, 'You're right. It's not even scuttling – it sounds more like galloping.'

I started visiting my friends and former neighbours more and more, and finding excuses not to go back before Peter was there. The area was considered 'nice'. We had friends literally down the road who had no trouble. Why was all this happening just to this house?

I told Peter, 'I think we should move.'

He said, 'It can't be like this all the time.'

'It *is* like this all the time.'

'It's just a bad patch. You've got an Aga. Give it a chance.'

Then, one night, we heard a dreadful noise. We ran out in our dressing gowns to see our car halfway through our neighbour's front gate. Something – evidently another car – had smashed into it so hard it had been pushed into next door's garden.

Our neighbour's reaction to our car in his garden was disconcerting; he was way too unshocked. The awful thought occurred to me that he was used to it. The car was a year old. And we had just bought it from Peter's firm.

I said, 'I want to move.'

'We'll make it better.'

'I can't stand it.'

'Let's see how it goes. You've got an Aga and a conservatory.'

'I don't give a shit about the conservatory! I hate it here!'

'But we've only been here two months.'

'OK. You stay at the Amityville Horror and see how it goes. I'm off.'

Finally he agreed, and I went back to the agent who'd sold our previous house. For the next two months I did nothing but try to sell this place and find another. I rang sixty estate agents every week, and mentioned it to anyone I thought might have a use for it, particularly as a business premises. At least that way they'd never have to stay the night. No one did, but doing something made us feel better. And I told a friend of Peter's, a property developer. Eventually a contact of his turned up, who knew the place already.

He looked round briefly, said, 'I used to play here as a child,' and made an offer.

We had nowhere to move to.

A week later, we were coming back from a friend's

birthday dinner. I went inside while Peter put the car away, and when he came to the door, his shirt was torn.

'What's happened?' I said. 'Where's your jacket?'

'I've been mugged.' He was breathing hard. Two men had put their hands over his face. They'd got his wallet, but not the car, even though he was standing there holding the keys.

'I think they were quite stupid. Either that or they didn't like Alfas.'

'I wish it had been me. I was the one who found this bloody place.'

'In a way,' he said, 'I'm glad.'

'*Glad?* Why?!'

'Because now I know I want to go. I have no more doubts.'

I redoubled my efforts to find somewhere else, looking at everything from an English Heritage restored mini mansion to a two-bedroomed flat above an exhaust centre. By the time I moved onto what we could afford to rent, the exhaust centre was starting to look good. One day, with time running out, we went to see a friend of Peter's, miles away on the other side of town.

'You should come and live down here,' he said. And looking at his lovely garden, with the absence of traffic noise or joyriders or drug dealers, we thought: *Why not?*

And just like that, we fell in love – with the house, the street and the whole thing.

'It may be South London,' I said, 'but it's *gorgeous!*'

His wife wasn't amused. 'You'll never get a house here,' she said. 'They always change hands privately.'

A few days later we were offered one in the same road.

So *nyeah*.

'So what have we learned from this experience?' I say to Peter.

'That reason and emotion *can* work together. Emotion makes you react, but reason gets you out of the situation.'

'When the going gets tough, the tough – run away . . .!'

'Absolutely!'

And I think that maybe, being a Grown-up means not being helpless. Maybe it's that simple. And that should really be the end of this book.

Except . . .

One day, as we are driving along, Lydia says: 'X's mummy slapped me in the car.'

And I say, '*What???!*'

And I quiz her and make her go over it three times to see if the story changes, and it doesn't. I remember the day. Lydia had gone over to play. And she said something silly to her friend's very religious mother, something anti-God, which offended her so much that she slapped her. I believe Lydia. So I have to speak to this woman. Only I'm *scared*. I've sold the Amityville Horror, and buried my father, and survived a car accident and finished two long-term relationships with entirely innocent men. But this fills me with dread. Yet if I do nothing, Lydia will have been let down and may never confide in me again. But *me*! I'm no good at this stuff!

Peter! He can do it. He's good at this. He's managed people. He's even had to sack one or two, which is surely just the *worst*. But he says nothing. Yet I want Lydia to know I'm on her side, that she can tell me things, that they can be dealt with. And, if I show her I can do this, maybe she'll grow up to be braver than me.

Right. I'm going to ask this woman if she slapped my daughter. No, hang on. Am I asking? Or *telling*? Perhaps something will happen that will let me off. An earthquake.

So – with no idea what I'm going to say – I ring her

number and, to my great relief, she's not in. But then I see her, pushing her younger one past the shops.

'Go in there and look at the books,' I tell Lydia. 'And I'll be there in a minute.'

The woman sees me, and I remember something Lawrence said once: 'Is it a real minute or a Bad Mother Minute? Because they're really long.' He wasn't being funny either. I think this might be a *very* long minute. One of the longest, indeed, of recent years. I remind myself that Lydia needs me to stand by her and that I am a Grown-up, even though I feel about three. If only I was Philip Marlowe. He didn't put things off, at least not for longer than it took to finish a cigarette. If this was *The Big Sleep* . . .

I parked and walked back. In the daylight it seemed an exposed and dangerous thing to do. The hedge at the front had fresh green leaves after the rain. In the cool morning light I could see the path that led to the park. Something moved behind the hedge as I drew level. A woman in a raincoat, pushing a stroller. She pushed faster, pretending she hadn't seen me. She didn't do a bad job of it, either.

'I'm in rather a hurry. You'll have to come back tomorrow.'

'I like now better.'

'Lydia's talked to me about what happened in the car when she came to play that time.'

'I don't remember anything happening.'

So I tell her.

And she says: 'Of course I didn't!'

What now, Marlowe? Well, what did I expect her to say?

'Um, well, Lydia said you did.'

'Of course I didn't. I wouldn't.'

I have no vocabulary for dealing with this. I might as well be in Japan.

She tipped her head slightly on one side. I assumed someone had once told her it looked cute.

And then she says: 'I may have given her a *tap* for being noisy in the car, but never a *slap*.'

Ah.

The difference between a tap and a slap. She wanted it to be just wide enough to step into and hide for a while. For as long as it took.

'You know what it's like, when they're all screaming at once.'

'Well, yes. But . . .'

'Look, honestly, I really don't remember. It's obviously a misunderstanding.'

It's like the dream where you're in the play with no script. I'm putting one foot in front of the other in the dark. But I defend Lydia, feeling in some primitively old-fashioned way that it's my job.

'Look, if I could just talk to Lydia,' she says. 'We could clear this up.'

'Talk to her with a 45 in your hand.' I'd seen those talks before.

And just as she says this, Lydia comes back out.

'You said you were coming in a minute.'

And she was there again, in the same navy pinafore and the same blonde hair. And the same brown eyes, deep enough to lose yourself in.

'I am, Lyd,' I say.

And then the woman says, 'I'm sorry, Lydia, I'm really sorry, if I did anything you *thought* was a slap, but you know I didn't, don't you?'

And she suddenly lifts her right into the air and squeezes her, ostensibly in a friendly way. *Friendly like a grizzly bear.* So I say, 'The thing is, you've got to understand that some people have different views from you, and she is, after all, seven.'

And she says, 'Don't you say that to me! I don't like being accused!'

'I wasn't there, of course. But you see my position? I can't believe both of you. What would you do?'

'What does that matter? It's clearly a misunderstanding.'

'I don't accept that. The thing is,' I say, 'I have to put my relationship with Lydia first.'

And she says, 'I don't care about your relationship with Lydia!'

And then she walks away.

And Lydia bursts into tears.

Lydia hates people seeing her cry, which is a tricky one because we're in the street. So I wait there, hiding her face in my chest until she stops.

I held her there until she'd finished, then we walked back to where I'd left the car under a pepper tree.

'Thanks,' she said. 'You're all right.'

I got in, started the engine and let out a deep breath.

'I'm going downtown,' I said. 'If you need a lift.'

After this I have trouble getting the incident out of my mind. But Lydia obviously feels better. She's handed the burden to me and I've picked it up, which is as it should be. Maybe parenting is one long relay race in which your children run up and give you all the difficult stuff. Then, as they get older, you start not picking up so much of it. Otherwise *they* never grow up. Could that be right? Maybe.

It was a crisp morning, with just enough snap in the air to make life seem simple and sweet, if you didn't have too much on your mind. I had.

While I am still fretting over this whole thing,

turning it over in my mind and trying to think what I would have done differently – if anything – Lydia starts her Annual Birthday Preparations. She's got her guest list out; there are only eight months to go. And the second name she puts on it is the daughter of this woman.

And I say, 'Hmm. Well, OK. Are you sure? Because of – you know, what happened with her mum.'

And *she* says, 'Mummy, that pony's galloped away.'

And I say, 'Eh? You mean—'

'That ship has sailed.'

'Blimey. Where did you get *that* from?'

'Syndrome in *The Incredibles*. It means that day has passed.'

I think about this. I think about it a lot. And all I can say is, I shall really have to try to be more like her.

Acknowledgments

I'd like to thank the extraordinary Mark Lucas, whose faith in me invariably outstrips the result.

George Morley, who gave me some ticks and a vg *and* made me laugh.

Peter, who read each draft of every chapter *and* did almost all the childcare.

My mother, Pat McNeill, who has always told me what anyone trying to be funny needs to hear.

My sister Claire, whose emails are the funniest things on my desk.

Lawrence and Lydia, for understanding why I have to disappear upstairs for hours at a time, i.e. to pay for more My Little Ponies and Bionicles.

Jon Stock at *Weekend Telegraph*, under whose excellent editorship parts of this book first appeared.

Katarina, Hugo, Vicky and Marieke, without whom we would never be able to go out, and I would be even *more* difficult to live with.

Jessica Chappell and Joe Moran, for sleepovers, science and sticky chicken, and making me laugh.

Dee, Sarah, Patrick, Ritchye, Amanda, Ursula, Lucy, Lisa, the Norths and anyone who ever offered to have the children to play so I could be a Typer.

Ruby, who gave me tea and sympathy in N1.

The sales team at Macmillan, for introducing me to the novel experience of actually selling books as opposed to just writing them.

Rebecca Lewis, who's worth four chocolates at least.

Larry, whose original instincts were sound.

The contributors to the Bad Mothers Club, whose work I am proud to publish.

Jo Hage, Julia Porter, Fiona Richardson and the moderators, who've done more than anyone will ever know – luckily for me.

Sophie Doyle, the Super PA who likes a challenge – which is just as well.

Jay Nagley, Tony Slack, Kathryn Lamb and Tony Legge, who keep the Bad Mothers Club from grinding to a halt while I am being a Typer.

The Bad Mothers themselves, who demonstrate daily that you cannot overestimate the value of moral support. The people at Grove Road, Bristol.

Raymond Chandler, who's inspired me for thirty years, though reading this you might wonder how.

Acknowledgements

Florence King, author of *Confessions of a Failed Southern Lady*, the first and still the best.

And my father, whose advice I still take.